D0933651

STRATEGIES FOR COMPETITIVE VOLLEYBALL

STEPHEN D. FRASER

Leisure Press
Champaign, Illinois

To my mom and dad for all the years of love and caring.

To my wife Lisa, without whose support and understanding this book would never have been completed.

Developmental Editor: June I. Decker, PhD
Copy Editor: Wendy Nelson
Assistant Editors: JoAnne Hutchcraft Cline and Christine Drews
Production Director: Ernie Noa
Projects Manager: Lezli Harris
Typesetter: Yvonne Winsor
Text Design: Keith Blomberg
Text Layout: Gretchen Walter
Cover Design: Jack Davis
Cover Photo: B. Hazelton–Focus West
Printed By: BookCrafters
Illustrations By: Stephen D. Fraser with the exception of the following done by Clare Huck: Figures 1.3, 4.13, 4.14, 4.19, 4.20, 4.21, 4.22, 4.23, 4.24, 4.25, 4.26, 4.27, 4.28, 4.29, 4.30, 4.31, 4.32 and 4.33.

ISBN: 0-88011-304-9

Library of Congress Cataloging-in-Publication Data
Fraser, Stephen D., 1961–
     Strategies for competitive volleyball / Stephen D. Fraser.
          p.   cm.
     Bibliography: p.
     ISBN 0-88011-304-9
     1. Volleyball.   2. Volleyball—Coaching.   I. Title.
     GV1015.3.F73   1988
     796.32′5—dc19   87-31853
                                                                                        CIP

Printed in the United States of America

10 9 8 7 6 5 4 3 2 1

Leisure Press
A Division of Human Kinetics Publishers, Inc.
Box 5076, Champaign, IL 61820
1-800-342-5457
1-800-334-3665 (in Illinois)

Contents

PREFACE   v

CHAPTER 1   BASICS   1

The Court   1
Legend   2
Player Positioning   3
Phases of Play   7

CHAPTER 2   OFFENSIVE SERVE   13

Location of Serve   14
Position of Players   18

CHAPTER 3   SERVE RECEPTION   31

W Serve Reception Formation   32
Cup Serve Reception Formation   51

CHAPTER 4   OFFENSE   71

The First Pass   71
Basic Offensive Attacks   77
Offensive Sets—The High Sets   81

Offensive Sets—The Quick Sets   85
Multiple Offense   96
Offensive Systems   104
Attack Coverage   113
Attack Coverage for the 6 Up Defense   116
Attack Coverage for the 6 Back Defense   120

CHAPTER 5   DEFENSE   **125**

Frontcourt Play   125
Backcourt Play   136
Defensive Team Play—6 Up and 6 Back Systems   139
Variations of the 6 Back Defensive System   151
Free Ball Defense   169

CHAPTER 6   THE SOUTHPAW SYSTEM   **177**

The Conventional Systems   178
The Southpaw System   179
The Southpaw System in Play   182

EPILOGUE   **191**

GLOSSARY   **193**

FURTHER READING   **197**

ABOUT THE AUTHOR   **198**

Preface

As the title suggests, this book deals with strategies and team tactics involved in the game of volleyball. It is not an instructional book on how to execute the various skills required to play volleyball. That is best left to the numerous books and films that have been produced solely for that purpose.

Instead, this book will endeavor to detail and explain basic tactics and strategies involved in volleyball team play. Few other volleyball books have given more than scant attention to this essential area of the game. It is certainly important that volleyball players possess strong individual skills. However, volleyball is not an individual's game; it is a team oriented game. Furthermore, it is a team game that requires very precise movement within a relatively confined area. It is therefore of the utmost importance that all players on the court have an understanding of exactly what their functions are—within the framework of a team. Perhaps it is even more important that players go beyond this to understand the strategic logic associated with their various functions within the team concept.

The coaches, players, and teachers who read this book will be given an unparalleled insight into the game of volleyball. Each of the following chapters deals with major areas of team play while investigating tactics and strategies that may be employed in any number of game situations. This is not to say, however, that the division of chapters separates any one component of the game from the others. All facets of the game of volleyball are, in one way or another, interdependent. This book has been compiled in a manner that should most easily differentiate, as well as interlock, the various strategical components inherent in volleyball team play.

Finally, this book will present a unique and heretofore rarely implemented style of play, "The Southpaw System." This is a system of play that I have advocated for years as a tactical alternative to the conventional systems in which setters set from the right third of the offensive court. If this chapter does nothing more than open the mind of the reader to the alternatives available beyond those of conventional volleyball, then it has served its purpose well.

Whether you are a coach, player, or teacher, this book will enlighten you as well as give you an enhanced appreciation of the finer points and complexities of the game of volleyball.

Chapter 1

Basics

Volleyball is a game requiring the combined skills of a number of individuals within the framework of a team. If a team is to be successful, it is essential that the skills of these individuals be utilized in an effective manner. This can be accomplished, however, only if both the coach and the players fully understand the concepts related to the overall functioning of the team. It is therefore initially imperative that the coach (or teacher) have a comprehensive understanding of the concepts affiliated with team play. These concepts must then be imparted to each player within the team structure. With a sound understanding of the concepts of team play, each player will be best prepared to fulfill his or her role within the framework of the team. In order for them to develop such comprehensive understanding, however, players first must have a knowledge of the basic elements upon which the game of volleyball has been developed.

The Court

The volleyball court is a rectangular playing surface composed of two square areas joined at the center line (Figure 1.1). Figure 1.2

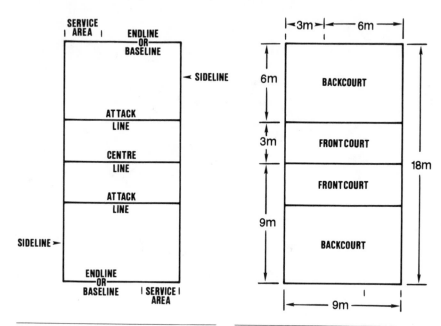

Figure 1.1 Labels and designations of prominent court boundaries.

Figure 1.2 Designation of court areas and dimensions of court boundaries.

illustrates the exact dimensions of these two square areas and the rectangle they form together. Figure 1.2 illustrates the dimensions of the volleyball court, and Figure 1.1 labels the boundaries and prominent markings. It is evident in Figure 1.1 that each playing area is identical to the other, not only in dimension but in designation also. The center line in fact divides the court into two distinctive playing areas, each of which is to be occupied by one team only. The connecting area, and ultimately the area through which all attacks must pass, is that area along the center line. Figure 1.3 illustrates the dimensions of the net, which extends along the length of the center line. The net provides the most tangible division between the two playing courts.

Legend

In an effort to simplify understanding of the following illustrations, it may be necessary to refer to the Legend (Figure 1.4).

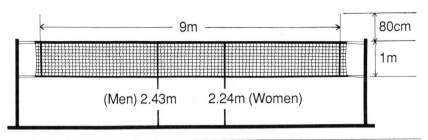

Figure 1.3 Dimensions of the net, which extends along the center line separating the two playing courts. Note the difference in height between the net for men and the net for women.

Player Positioning

Volleyball, like most team sports, is a game with a number of rules for the positioning of players in various circumstances. These rules govern the positioning of individual players in relation both to the playing court and to other teammates. Following is a brief overview of some of the positioning restrictions and the instances in which they are applicable.

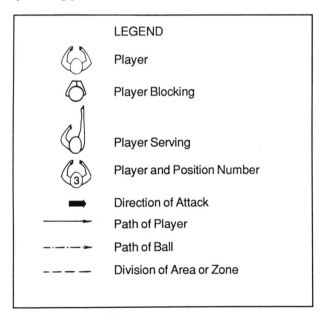

Figure 1.4 A key to understanding the symbols that are used throughout the following chapters.

Rotational Order

There are six players on each of the two playing courts at any given time, and there are likewise six zones of the volleyball court in which these players may be positioned. These six zones are designated numerically to ensure simplicity. Figure 1.5 illustrates these six zones of the court and the players positioned within them. The numbering of these zones begins with the server's corner of the court and progresses numerically, counterclockwise, #1 through #6. The numbering of these positions, referred to as the *rotational order*, serves as a guide to the rotation of players within the court. Following a side out, all players rotate one position clockwise, progressively through the numerical hierarchy.

The rotational order provides a simplified system for identifying the initial positioning of players through each of the six possible rotations. Players in the #2, #3, and #4 positions are frontcourt players and players in the #5, #6, and #1 positions are backcourt players. Furthermore, players in the #3 and #6 positions are in the middle of their respective front- and backcourt teammates. This rotational order remains constant regardless of the rotation of players. Accordingly, throughout a particular sequence of play, all players are referred to by the number of their initial positions within the rotational order prior to the beginning of that play. This makes

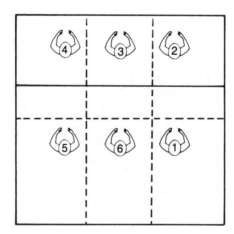

Figure 1.5 The numerical designation of the court and of the players located within those zones.

it possible to understand and follow the movement of players following an offensive serve or a serve reception.

Before an offensive serve or a serve reception, however, all players are required to remain within the bounds of their positions in the rotational order. To do so, all players must maintain their positions with respect to lateral positioning and frontcourt/backcourt positioning.

Lateral Positioning

Lateral positioning refers to the initial alignment of players' positioning in relation to their respective frontcourt and backcourt teammates. Figure 1.6 illustrates the basic positioning of the six players within the rotational order. Laterally, in the frontcourt, player #3 must remain between players #4 and #2, player #4 must remain to the left of player #3, and player #2 must remain in a position to the right of player #3. In the backcourt, player #6 must maintain a position laterally between players #5 and #1, player #5 must remain to the left of player #6, and player #1 must remain to the right of player #6.

Figure 1.7 illustrates a somewhat unlikely situation in which the six players all retain their positions within the rotational order according to these requirements. In terms of lateral positioning, the

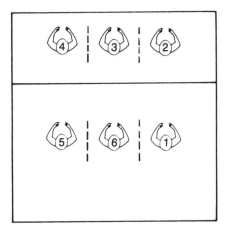

Figure 1.6 Basic alignment of the six players with respect to lateral positioning in both the front- and the backcourt.

Figure 1.7 An example of one possible alignment of the six players with respect to lateral positioning.

frontcourt and backcourt players are independent, and Figure 1.7 illustrates the fact that backcourt players are not required to remain in a position behind their frontcourt counterparts. However, although the front- and backcourt players are independent laterally, there is a positional requirement that must be mutually observed by both the front- and backcourt players.

The positioning laws require that each backcourt player maintain a position behind his or her respective frontcourt counterpart.

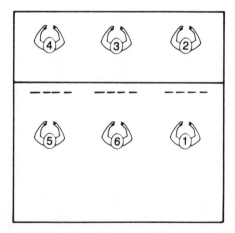

Figure 1.8 Basic alignment of the six players with respect to frontcourt/backcourt positioning.

Basically this means that the backcourt players must not be in initial positions closer to the net than their frontcourt counterparts, irrespective of lateral positioning. Therefore, player #5 must remain behind player #4, player #6 must remain behind player #3, and player #1 must remain behind player #2. This is illustrated basically in Figure 1.8. Figure 1.9 illustrates this same positioning in a somewhat altered and uncommon alignment. Nevertheless, all backcourt players have remained in positions behind their respective frontcourt counterparts. It should be further noted that all six players have also mantained their lateral positionings in this alignment. As a result, the positional integrity of this alignment remains within the legal limitations of positioning prior to an offensive serve or a serve reception.

Figure 1.9   An example of one possible alignment of the six players with respect to frontcourt/backcourt positioning.

Phases of Play

There are four basic phases of play within the construct of a volleyball game. These four phases of play are offensive serve, serve reception, offense, and defense. Of these four phases of play, however, both offense and defense can be further reduced. Each of these two phases of play is the result of the combination of multiple components. The offensive phase is the result of the combination of preparation of offense, execution of attack, and attack coverage. The defensive phase is the result of the combination of preparation of defense and execution of defense. All of the four basic phases of play are unique, yet none are mutually exclusive of the others.

The nature of the game is based not only on the rotary movement of players within each of the two court areas but also on the cyclical rotation of the phases of play. These phases of play will move in two distinct cycles, dependent upon whether play has begun for your team with an offensive serve or a serve reception. Figure 1.10 illustrates the cycle of the phases of play if your team were responsible for initiating play with an offensive serve. Figure 1.11 illustrates the cycle should your team be in a serve reception situation. In each of these cycles, the components of both offense and defense are present. The differentiating factor, however, is the direction of rotary movement through the cycle. In the case where the offensive serve is the initial phase, movement is from the defensive phase to the offensive phase (Figure 1.10); when serve reception is the initial phase, movement is from the offensive phase to the defensive phase (Figure 1.11). To better understand each of these cycles, it is necessary first to understand each of the phases of play and the components inherent in them.

Figure 1.10   The cycle of the phases of play beginning with the offensive serve and moving through defense to offense, etc.

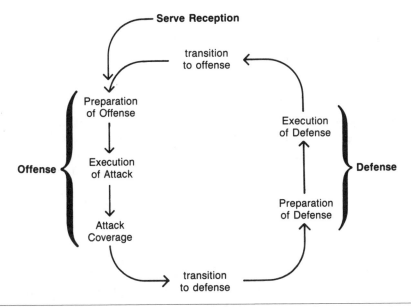

Figure 1.11 The cycle of the phases of play beginning with serve reception and moving through offense to defense, etc.

Offensive Serve

This phase of play occurs during a dead ball situation. In this situation there is a substantial amount of time for players of the serving team to prepare their subsequent defense of the opposition's attack. This includes specific positioning prior to the serve, followed by movement to a predetermined area at the time of the serve.

Serve Reception

Serve reception is also a phase of play that arises from a dead ball situation. In this case, the priority for the receiving team is to position players in an alignment conducive to both receiving the serve and executing an attack following the successful reception of the serve.

Offense

The phase of play known as offense is the umbrella for three distinct components: preparation of attack, execution of attack, and attack coverage. These components are inherently interdependent elements of the offensive phase of play. However, all are distinctly independent in objective and execution.

Preparation of Attack

Following serve reception or the transition from defense, the offensive players position themselves in areas from which the attack could be executed. The setter moves to the frontcourt setter's position while each hitter moves to his or her frontcourt preattack position.

Execution of Attack

This component of the offensive phase includes the actual pass from the setter, the approach of the attackers, and the subsequent contact of the ball by the hitter. It is at this time that the ball is directed toward the opponent's court area.

Attack Coverage

During the offensive attack it is necessary to be prepared to play the ball should it be blocked by the opposition back into your court area. Therefore, a specific alignment of positions is required of the nonhitting players. This in effect is preparatory to the transition to defense.

Transition to Defense

This is the period when a team must redirect its focus from offense to defense. During this period the opposition has control of the ball, giving your team time to recover from the offensive attack and position itself defensively. This transition leads to the preparation of the defense component of the defensive phase of play.

Defense

The defensive phase of play as a whole is comprised of two lesser components: preparation of defense and execution of defense.

Preparation of Defense

While the opposition is in possession of the ball, it is necessary to position defensively and prepare for the onset of the opposition's offensive attack. This requires anticipating the attack of the opposition by preparing both a frontcourt block and specific positioning of the three backcourt players.

Execution of Defense

This component of the defensive phase of play involves actual defense of the opposition's attack. At this time a defensive block is executed by the appropriate frontcourt player(s) while the backcourt players attempt to defensively save the attacked ball.

Transition to Offense

Following the successful defense of the opposition's attack, it is necessary to make the transition from defense to offense. This transition leads naturally into the preparation of offense component of the offensive phase of play.

With a basic understanding of each of these phases of play and their respective components, it will now be possible to delve into the specifics of each. Chapters 2 through 5 each deal specifically with one of these four phases of play. Although each phase of play is dealt with in a separate chapter, it should be remembered that they are not mutually exclusive. All are interdependent in the cyclical pattern of play within the game structure.

Chapter 2

Offensive Serve

The offensive serve is that juncture of the game when your team has possession of the ball in a dead ball situation and must resume play by serving to the opposition. In a sense, the term *offensive serve* is a misnomer. It is true that because your team has possession of the ball, you are in an offensive position. However, it is inherent in beginning play with a serve that your team will in fact be relinquishing possession of the ball without an offensive attack. In actuality you will be passing the ball to the opposition, thereby placing your team in a defensive position.

In light of the importance of the serve, it is essential that the coach determine a strategy that will counterbalance the offensive disadvantages inherent in the serve. To this end, a two-pronged strategy must be employed. One element of this strategy, which is offense oriented, is *location of the serve*. This simply means serving the ball to a player or area that will most disadvantage the receiving team. The second, more defensive, element of this strategy is *positioning of players*. This refers to the realignment of players during the serve, thus allowing the greatest number of defensive and offensive possibilities for the serving team. These two elements of strategy are of extreme importance to the ultimate success of the offensive serve, and therefore they must be analyzed so that both the coach and player have a thorough understanding of the practical applications of this strategy.

Location of Serve

This is the offensive element of the offensive service strategy. By serving to specific players or areas, you can exploit weaknesses of the receiving team that will ultimately affect the opposition's ability to execute an offensive attack.

Serving to Specific Players

Following are three possible options to be considered when choosing to serve to specific players.

Serving to a Poor Receiver/Passer

As a result of scouting, previous meetings, or simply watching the opposition, it should be evident who is the weakest receiver/passer on the opposing team. Once this has been established, it may be advisable to serve the ball to this lesser skilled player. The anticipated result would be a mishandled serve reception or a poor pass to the setter. Often, if lesser skilled players mishandle a serve, they will then be much less confident and accordingly less able to receive second serves to their areas. Therefore, it is advised that the serving team continue to serve to the weakest receiver on the opposing team. Should that player be substituted for, in an attempt to eliminate the receiving weakness, another opportunity for the serving team will still arise.

Serving to a Substitute Player

If the receiving team has a recent substitute or a bench player on the court, it is often useful to serve to that person. In many cases substitutes have been sparingly exposed to game situations and are unable to react optimally when pressed into action. In almost all cases substitutes come into a game relatively cold, without a thorough warm up, which significantly diminishes their ability to react and move quickly. Hence, it is advisable to take advantage of a substitute's lack of game experience and lack of warm-up to create the possibility of a mishandled reception or a poorly executed pass to the setter.

Serving to a Penetrating Setter

When serving to a team whose backcourt setter is penetrating to the frontcourt, it can be very advantageous to force the penetrating setter to receive the serve. Although it is technically difficult for the server to serve to a point along the setter's path to the frontcourt, it is very effective to force the penetrating setter to receive the ball. If successful, it would be necessary for a frontcourt player to take on the role of setter. This in itself reduces the number of eligible hitters by at least one, thereby limiting the offensive possibilities of the opposing team. Furthermore, it disturbs the flow of the opposition's offense by reducing their ability to execute a planned attack using a penetrating setter.

Serving to Specific Areas

When choosing to serve to specific areas, there are four theoretical options that are useful in determining exactly which area may be exploited most successfully.

Serving to the Deep Corner Areas

It is potentially productive to serve the ball to either of the two deep corner areas (Figure 2.1). In order for the opposition to receive a ball served in either of these two areas, the receiving player must move laterally to that corner. In doing so, the receiver is moving away from the setter frontcourt position. If a pass is then to be made to the setter, it must be executed in a direction opposite to the direction of movement of the receiving player. This will result in a very difficult and often inaccurate pass to the frontcourt setter. The desired end result is that the setter is forced to move out of position to receive a poor pass, thus limiting the offensive posibilities available to the hitters.

Serving to the Sideline Areas

In this situation the receiving player is again moving away from the frontcourt setter when he or she contacts the ball. Again too, the possibility of a poor first pass to the setter is increased. A service to the sidelines also allows the additional possibility that the receiver will not attempt to receive the ball at all, believing that the serve is traveling out of bounds. In light of this, it is also possible for the server to compound the illusion of the ball traveling out of the playing court.

Figure 2.2 illustrates both the left (a) and right (b) sideline areas to which the server may choose to direct the ball. When serving to the left (a) sideline area, a crosscourt serve is necessary. Because the serve is directed crosscourt, when it travels toward the left sideline area it will appear to the receiver to be traveling in a line out of bounds. In some cases the receiver will simply let the ball land untouched. If the server is accurate, the ball can land within the

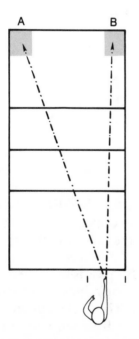

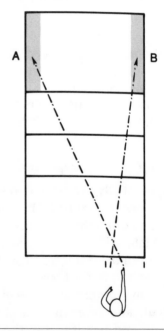

Figure 2.1 The two deep corner areas to which a serve may be directed.

Figure 2.2 The two sideline areas to which a serve may be directed. Note the server's initial position when serving to the right (b) sideline area.

court boundaries even though it appears to be heading out of bounds.

When serving to the right (b) sideline area, the server is serving the ball in a line almost parallel to the right sideline itself. This decreases the likelihood that the receiver will believe the ball to be traveling out of bounds. Instead, the server should move to the far left side of the server's area (Figure 2.2) and serve partially across the court in order to put the ball in the right (b) sideline area. Now the ball will be traveling in a line toward the out-of-bounds area. Once again, the possibility that the receiver will perceive the ball to be directed out of bounds has been greatly increased, and the possibility that the receiver will choose not to play the served ball increases proportionally.

Serving to the Short Attack Line Area

As is the case with the two previous areas, serving to the short attack line area (Figure 2.3) requires the receiving player to be moving when contacting the ball. In this instance, however, the receiver is not moving laterally. Instead he or she must move forward and in many cases will be lunging to dig up this short serve in order to keep the ball from contacting the floor. As it is necessary to move quickly to play this serve, the receiver's momentum and direction of movement will be forward toward the serving team.

Often receivers find it too difficult to pass the ball laterally to the setter and must instead pass according to their direction of body movement—back to the serving team. This creates an ideal opportunity for the serving team to exchange a one-contact serve for a one-contact reception. In this situation the advantage clearly reverts to the serving team, who may now execute a full three-contact offensive attack.

Serving to the Middle Area

Serving to the middle court area will be most effective when the opposing team is using a cup serve reception formation (see chapter 3). This formation involves four players in a semicircle or cup formation. Because there are no players positioned in the middle of the court, the obvious area of susceptibility is the unprotected middle court area. Figure 2.4 illustrates this middle area, around which the four receiving players would be positioned.

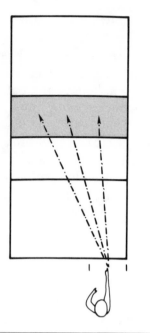

Figure 2.3 The short attack line area to which a serve may be directed.

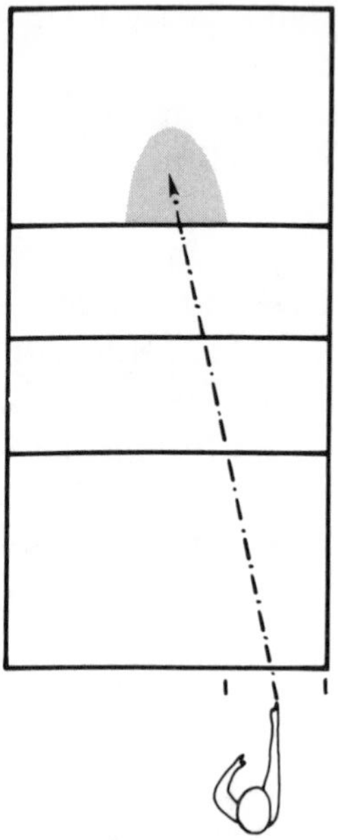

Figure 2.4 The middle court area to which a serve may be directed when serving to a team using a cup serve reception formation.

The anticipated result of this serve is an all-or-none receiving effort. That is, either nobody attempts to receive the serve, each player thinking it is the responsibility of someone else, or two or more players believe it to be their responsibility and attempt to receive the serve. In either case, the opposition's possible lack of knowledge or experience is exploited to the advantage of the serving team.

Position of Players

Once the ball has been served, the serving team must be prepared both to defend the opposition's attack and, following that, to formulate an offensive attack of its own. In order to most effectively prepare for this, the serving team must be positioned in a manner that offers the greatest potential for success. Because the positioning of players is different on each rotation, it is necessary for players to switch to positions in which they are most effective both defensively and offensively.

Unquestionably, the most convenient time for the serving team players to switch is during the offensive serve. The ball must travel to the opposition's court and must then be played a minimum of one time before an attack must be defended. This gives the serving team a great deal of time in which to switch positions.

Guidelines When Switching Player Positions

For the most part, switching during the serve is lateral only. Were backcourt players to switch into the frontcourt, they would be unable to legally block an attack. This would severely hamper the defensive possibilities of the serving team. Therefore, with very few exceptions, switching will be lateral and mutually exclusive in both the front- and backcourt (Figure 2.5). There are, however, several important guidelines that should be adhered to when endeavoring to switch player positioning during the offensive serve.

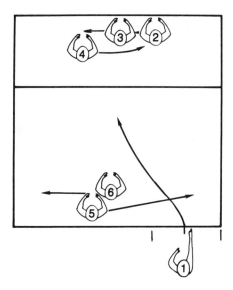

Figure 2.5 A situation in which all players are involved in a switch.

Attentiveness to Opposition

All players on the serving team (excluding the server) should have their attention focused on the opposition rather than on their own serving player. It is important that each player continually observe the alignment and movement of the opposition's receivers. There should also always be one player at the net who is responsible for locating the opposition's eligible hitters. Often it will be the responsibility of the frontcourt outside hitter to locate these eligible hitters and notify his or her teammates. Locating the opposition's attackers will make it possible for the frontcourt blockers to concentrate only on the eligible hitters rather than on possible fake hitters.

Proximity to Positions

All players involved in a position switch should attempt to minimize the distance they must travel in order to arrive at their intended positions. This decreases the length of time spent moving and increases the length of time the player has to prepare for the opposition's attack. Players should move as close as possible to their intended positions, within the limits of legal player positioning, and be aware of their positions prior to the service to be sure that they are not out of rotation. It is necessary to minimize the distance to be traveled, but not so much so that the integrity of player positioning is jeopardized.

Frontcourt Preparedness

Should a situation arise in which all three frontcourt players must switch, at least two players must remain close to the net throughout the switch. Figure 2.6 illustrates one such situation. Here, both players #2 and #3 move in the same direction and thus remain close to the net during the position switch. Player #4, the only player moving in the opposite direction, switches laterally behind players #2 and #3 to avoid any possible collision. At least two players must remain close to the net to be in a position to block, should the opposition mount a quick offensive attack.

Cue to Switch

As has been discussed, the nonserving players should have their attention focused on the opposition during the serve. Therefore, these players must listen for the sound of the server's contact with

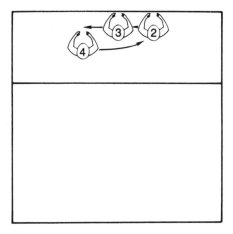

Figure 2.6 All three frontcourt players switching while ensuring that at least two players remain close to the net.

the ball. Upon hearing this contact, all switching players immediately move to their intended positions. Should a situation arise where it is impossible for the players to hear the contact of the ball (e.g., excessive crowd noise), then the server provides a verbal cue to switch. Immediately following contact of the ball, the server shouts "serve" or "switch," following which the switching players start moving to their intended positions.

Determining Intended Player Positions

Although there are many different offensive systems (see chapter 4), almost every system includes two players who are delegated as possible setters, two players who are delegated as possible middle hitters, and two players who are delegated as possible outside hitters. To simplify the following discussion, players delegated as setters will be labeled S, players delegated as middle hitters will be labeled M, and players delegated as outside hitters will be labeled H.

When determining intended player positioning, one must first break the court down into three parallel lanes (Figure 2.7). Each of these lanes (a), (b), and (c) will become a designated area of intended positioning for each individual player in both the front- and backcourt. Figure 2.7 illustrates the intended positions of the three frontcourt players: the outside hitter in lane (a), the middle hitter

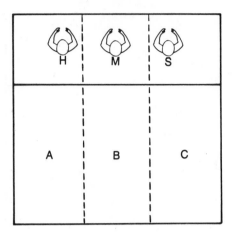

Figure 2.7   The three parallel lanes in which the outside hitter (H), the middle hitter (M), and the setter (S) are positioned.

in lane (b), and the setter in lane (c). As these are the intended positions for frontcourt players, the outside hitter (H), middle hitter (M), and setter (S) are required to move to their respective positions immediately following the serve. These intended positions remain the same irrespective of the particular rotation in which the serving team may be. In essence, the intended positioning of the frontcourt players will always be like that diagramed in Figure 2.7.

The intended positioning of the backcourt players, however, will depend upon the type of defensive system to be employed. There are basically two types of defensive systems, the 6 back and the 6 up. The 6 back system is one in which player #6 plays back in a position close to the baseline while players #5 and #1 are positioned in areas close to the attack line in the backcourt. Conversely, the 6 up system has player #6 in a position close to the attack line in the backcourt while players #5 and #1 are positioned in areas close to the baseline.

Intended Positions When Using the 6 Back Defense

When the 6 back defensive system is to be used, there are two possibilities for the intended positioning of the backcourt players (Figures 2.8 and 2.9). Figure 2.8 illustrates the most basic of the two possibilities. In this situation, the backcourt players are aligned in the same lateral positions as are the frontcourt players while they maintain their positions within the 6 back defensive system.

From a position close to the attack line, the backcourt setter (S) can penetrate forward to set a free ball, thus allowing the frontcourt setter (S) to move off the net and become a third eligible hitter.

Figure 2.9 illustrates a similar alignment with the exception that the backcourt middle hitter (M) and outside hitter (H) have reversed

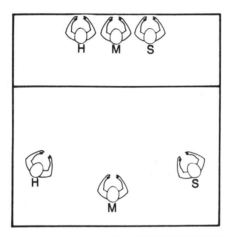

Figure 2.8 Intended positions of backcourt players when front- and backcourt lateral positions are identical.

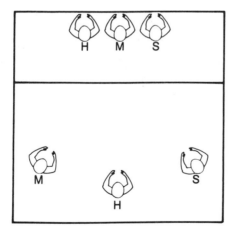

Figure 2.9   Intended positions of backcourt players when the middle hitter and outside hitter reverse positions for defensive purposes.

positions. This alignment is often used by teams having middle hitters who are, for the most part, limited in range and mobility and thus unable to adequately play the difficult 6 back position. Outside hitters usually are better all-around athletes than middle hitters, in terms of agility, mobility, and quickness, and therefore it is often necessary to have the outside hitters play the very demanding 6 back position. Ultimately, the decision to reverse the positions of the backcourt outside and middle hitters will be a result of defensive considerations. This reversal invariably improves the backcourt defense without causing any negative effects to the offense.

Intended Positions When Using the 6 Up Defense

When using the 6 up defensive system, there is only one recommended alignment for the intended positioning of the backcourt players. Figure 2.10 shows the position of the three backcourt players within the framework of the 6 up defensive system. At a glance it appears that the backcourt setter (S) and the middle hitter (M) are in the wrong positions. There is a very good reason, however, for this particular alignment. If playing in the deep corner area on defense (zone #1), the setter would be unable to set in a free ball situation because of the great distance he or she would have to travel to the frontcourt setter's position. Instead, by play-

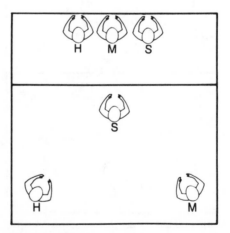

Figure 2.10 Intended positions of the three backcourt players when using the 6 up defensive system.

ing the 6 up position, the setter is placed very close to the front-court setter's position. As a result, in a free ball situation the backcourt setter can move forward to set, thereby allowing the front-court setter to move off the net and become a third eligible hitter.

Direction of Player Movement to Intended Positions

In order that all six players may effectively and efficiently arrive at their intended positions, a logical and well practiced routine of movement must be in place. The difficulty, of course, is that for each particular rotation and each particular defensive system being used, there is a particular pattern of movement that must correspond. Following is a detailed analysis of movement patterns for all appropriate rotations in three different defensive systems.

6 Back With Front- and Backcourt Players in Identical Lateral Positions

Figures 2.11 (i) through (ix) illustrates the initial positions [(i), (iv), and (vii)], directions of movement [(ii), (v), and (viii)], and final positioning of players [(iii), (vi), and (ix)] through each of the first three rotations (i.e., rotation of players following opponent's loss of serve). Only the initial three rotations need to be diagramed, as rotations four through six are simply repetitions of rotations one through three. It is evident immediately that the final positioning of players is identical in each of the three rotations [Figure 2.11 (iii), (vi), and (ix)]. This is consistent with the positioning of players in the 6 back defense when it is prudent to have the backcourt players in the same lateral positions as their frontcourt counterparts.

Because the initial positioning of players is different in each of the three rotations [Figure 2.11 (i), (iv), and (vii)], the direction of player movement must also be different. This is necessary if the final positioning of players is to be consistent with that of the 6 back defensive system. Figure 2.11 (ii), (vi), and (viii) illustrate the direction of player movement for each of the first three rotations.

It is important to note also that player movement in each of the three rotations adheres to the guidelines that apply when switching player positioning. In each case, the moving players begin in a position as close as possible to the position they will be moving

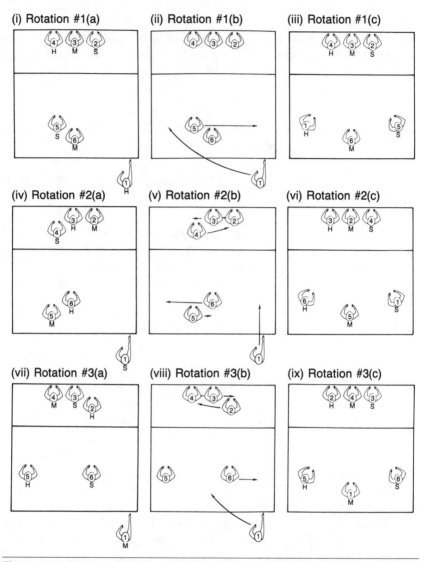

Figure 2.11 (i) - (ix) Initial positioning [(i), (iv), and (vii)], direction of movement [(ii), (v), and (viii)], and final positioning [(iii), (vi), and (ix)] of players through each of the first three rotations when using the 6 back defense with front- and backcourt players in identical lateral positions.

to. Perhaps more importantly, each player must begin in a position that is within the legal limits of player positioning prior to the serve. In each rotation there also must be at least two frontcourt players positioned at the net throughout the switching process. This ensures that an adequate block may be established, should the opposition choose to form a quick attack following their reception of the serve.

6 Back With Backcourt Outside and Middle Hitter Positions Reversed

As in the previous 6 back defensive alignment, the player movement within this defensive system adheres to the guidelines for player movement. A major difference between the two systems, however, is evident in the final positioning of players. Figure 2.12 (iii), (vi), and (ix) illustrates this final positioning. In each of the three rotations, the backcourt outside hitter is located in the 6 back position while the middle hitter is positioned behind the attack line near the left sideline area.

Although the initial positioning is the same in each respective rotation as in the previous 6 back system, in this system the final positioning is different. Therefore, the direction of player movement must also differ. Figure 2.12 (ii), (v), and (viii) illustrates the directions of player movement necessary to effect this final positioning of players. Here, as before, the responsibility for player movement is different in each of the three rotations. This is invariably necessary in order to ensure that the same final positioning will be reached irrespective of which rotation the team may be in.

6 Up

Unlike the situation when using the 6 back defense, there is only one option for final positioning when using the 6 up defensive system. Figure 2.13 (iii), (vi), and (ix) illustrates this final positioning. In this situation, the backcourt setter and backcourt middle hitter have reversed lateral positions, enabling the setter to be located in an area nearer to the frontcourt setter's position. This is necessary in order that the backcourt setter may be able to penetrate to the frontcourt and set in a free ball situation.

Just as the 6 up alignment for final player positioning differs from the 6 back alignment in both design and player responsibility, the direction of player movement also differs. Figure 2.13 (ii), (vi), and (viii) illustrates the direction of movement the players must adhere to in switching within the 6 up defensive system. In each of the three rotations, the switching players must again adhere to the same guidelines for player movement as apply to a 6 back defensive system. These guidelines produce the common element evident in

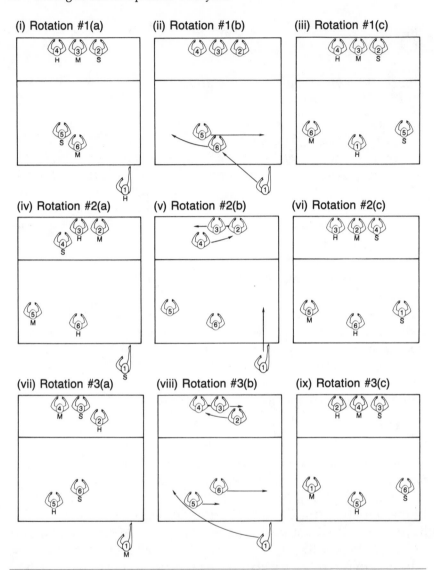

Figure 2.12 (i) - (ix) Initial positioning [(i), (iv), and (vii)], direction of movement [(ii), (v), and (viii)], and final positioning [(iii), (vi), and (ix)] of players through each of the first three rotations when using the 6 back defense with backcourt outside and middle hitter positions reversed.

every system in which switching occurs during the offensive serve, because they ultimately dictate the potential paths of player movement. Consequently, diagraming the resulting directions of player movement requires consulting and understanding these guidelines.

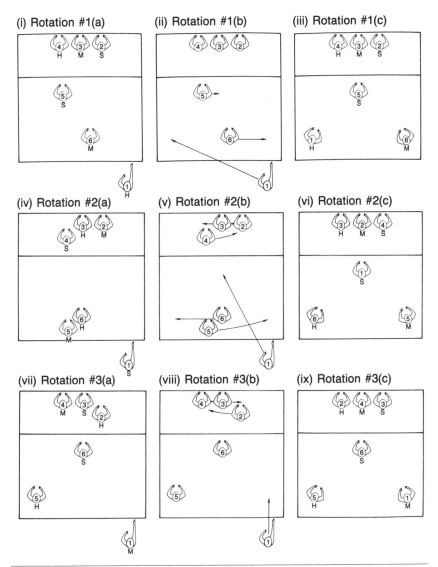

Figure 2.13 (i) - (ix) Initial positioning [(i), (iv), and (vii)], direction of movement [(ii), (v), and (viii)], and final positioning [(iii), (vi), and (ix)] of players
through each of the first three rotations when using the 6 up defense.

Chapter 3

Serve Reception

Perhaps the most crucial component of any team's offense is the ability to successfully receive the opposition's serve. Should the serve be poorly received, the possibility of executing a strong offensive attack is very diminished. Accordingly, the primary consideration of serve reception is to align the receiving players in such a manner that the served ball may be most easily received and accurately played to the setter upon the first pass. The secondary consideration is to have the receiving players aligned in such a manner that once the first pass has been made to the setter, the offense is in a position to execute a successful attack. Hence, there is an intrinsically defensive consideration, which is contrasted by an equally offensive consideration.

In response to this, there are two basic server reception formations: the *W formation* which adheres most closely to the defensive consideration, and the *cup formation*, which more closely serves the needs of the offensive consideration. This chapter will explore the W and the cup formations along with the multitude of positioning possibilities inherent in each. Because the primary consideration is defensive service reception, the initial discussion will focus on the W serve reception formation.

W Serve Reception Formation

The W serve reception formation is so called because of its resemblance to the letter W (Figure 3.1). In this serve reception formation five players are designated as service receivers. This means that one player is omitted as a service receiver. This nonreceiving player is in fact the designated setter. (The designated setter may be a frontcourt or backcourt penetrating setter and will be more fully discussed later in this chapter.) As a result, the five remaining players are positioned such that they are able to cover the largest area possible in order to satisfy the primary consideration of defense. This W serve reception formation is widely accepted as the more defensive of the two formations and as such is used by younger or less talented teams, especially teams that do not have highly skilled passers.

Player Positioning

The setter may be "hidden" in a number of areas, but the basic positioning of the three front and two back row players remains unchanged. Figure 3.2 illustrates the approximate positioning of these five receiving players in relation to the prominent court boundaries.

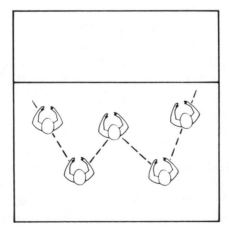

Figure 3.1 Basic positioning of players to form the W effect of this serve reception formation.

In the W serve reception formation, player B acts as the pivot around which players A, C, D, and E align themselves. (It should be noted that the letters A, B, C, D, and E are used in this discussion rather than the player position numbers. This is because any number of player combinations may occupy these positions and accurate player identification is not necessary to illustrate the spatial positioning of each of these five serve reception positions.) Player B is in a midcourt position approximately 5-6 feet behind the attack line. On either side of player B, players A and C position themselves somewhat closer to the attack line yet not so close that the basic straight line positioning of the three front row players is disturbed. Player A is in a position approximately 3-4 feet inside the sideline and 4-5 feet behind the attack line. In this position, player A can receive serves along the sideline as well as short soft serves inside the attack line area. Player C is positioned somewhat closer to the attack line (3-4 feet) but somewhat farther from the sideline (4-5 feet) than player A. Player C can afford to play farther from the sideline, due to the fact that most serves in this area are softer, higher arching serves as a result of the severe angle between this position and the server. Should a serve be directed toward the sideline, player C would have ample time to react and then get repositioned to receive the serve.

The backcourt players, D and E, position themselves such that any served ball approaching at or above shoulder level would travel out of bounds beyond the baseline. For the most part, this makes

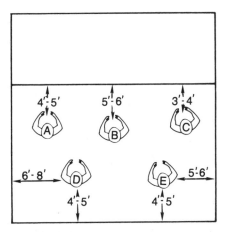

Figure 3.2 Position of the five receiving players in relation to the prominent court boundaries.

it necessary for them to position themselves approximately 4-5 feet inside the baseline. Laterally, players D and E position themselves approximately 6-8 feet and 5-6 feet inside their respective sidelines. This puts each in a position between and behind the three front row receivers. Not only does this positioning allow the backcourt players an unobstructed view of the server, but it effectively fills in any gaps in the overall team serve reception formation.

Player Responsibilities

Figure 3.3 illustrates the individual areas of reception responsibility for each of the five receiving players when passing to a setter in the right front position. Player B is responsible for the short middle area along with the area laterally between players A and C. Any served ball that is traveling at or above the shoulder level of player B must be played by either of the two backcourt players. Players A and C are responsible for the short area immediately behind player B and the short areas along each respective sideline. An additional responsibility of player A is to defend against the hard line serve. However, player A should receive line serves only when they can be played with a sure, underhand bump pass. If player A must reach up or behind to contact the ball, the ball should be received by the backcourt player D instead. This same rationale

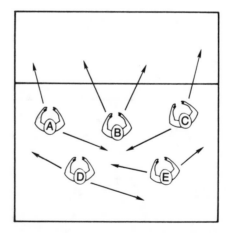

Figure 3.3 Areas of player responsibility when passing to a setter in the right front position.

also holds true for player C, should any serve be executed deeply crosscourt.

Player D is responsible for serves directed behind player A, deep serves to the corner area, and deep serves along the baseline laterally to player E. It is essential that player D receive these deep baseline serves intended laterally for player E, to ensure the greatest possibility for reception. Having player D receive these serves ensures that the receiver is moving toward the setter when passing the ball. This creates a greater potential for a successful pass than were player E to receive this serve because player E would be forced to make a pass to the setter (in the opposite direction) while moving away from the setter (a most undesirable circumstance for executing a pass).

Therefore, player E is concerned with the area along the right sideline, the deep corner area, and the deeper area behind and to the right of player B. For the most part, player E will receive the majority of serves during a game and must have an awareness of his or her responsibilities within the team reception structure. Having players aware of their areas of responsibility is perhaps the most significant factor in serve reception. In accord with this, players must be told not only where they are to cover but, more importantly, why.

Figure 3.4 illustrates how the functions of players D and E are completely reversed should the pass be directed to a setter in the

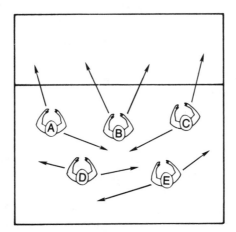

Figure 3.4 Areas of player responsibility when passing to a setter in the left front position.

left frontcourt position. The underlying principles for these responsibilities are the same as have been discussed. In conjunction with these principles, it is essential that the areas of responsibility also correspond to the new direction in which the received serve must be passed. This example further illustrates the need for players to fully understand the reasons that dictate their areas of responsibility. Without an understanding of the rationale, the mere positioning of players will not be sufficient to ensure team cohesion.

Penetration

Penetration refers to the action of a backcourt setter during the serve reception phase of play. In penetrating, the backcourt setter avoids receiving the opposition's serve and instead moves forward to set from the frontcourt area. The advantages here are twofold. First, the backcourt player you wish to delegate as penetrating setter does not have to be concerned with playing the opposition's serve, and second, it is now possible to make use of a three-hitter attack (see chapter 4) when the frontcourt setter is not required to set the offense.

The latter advantage is perhaps the most appealing in regard to its offensive potential. It is often useful to penetrate on most serve reception opportunities, as this penetration allows the receiving team to prepare a three-hitter attack. A three-hitter attack places a great deal of pressure on the defense and allows an unlimited number of offensive attack possibilities. The decision to implement a penetrating setter, however, will depend as much upon the skill level of the players involved as it will upon the strategic advantage it provides. Following are three examples of the most basic penetrations from each of the three frontcourt zones.

Player #1 Penetrating From Zone #2

In Figure 3.5, player #1 is the designated setter and as such is not in a position to receive the served ball. Player #1 is in fact hidden behind player #2, who will receive any ball served in that area. In this instance, player #1 is the penetrating setter. That is, as a backcourt player, player #1 will be penetrating to the frontcourt to set the first pass. Having a backcourt player set the ball allows the receiving team to utilize the three eligible hitters, players #4, #3,

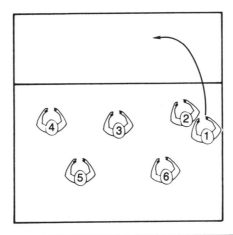

Figure 3.5 Player #1 penetrating to the frontcourt setter's position.

and #2. The crucial element in having the backcourt setter penetrate is retaining the integrity of player positioning prior to the serve.
Player #1 must be in a position behind player #2 prior to the serve.
Once the server has contacted the ball, player #1 may move ahead,
or penetrate, to the frontcourt setter's position.

It is also essential that player #1 start in a position to the right
of player #2 and penetrate along a lane also to the right of player
#2. In doing so, the penetrating setter (player #1) will not cross
through the line of vision of player #2. It is not only imperative
that the penetrating setter avoid receiving the ball but it is equally
imperative that the penetrating setter not interfere in his or her
teammate's reception of the serve.

Player #6 Penetrating From Zone #3

When penetrating from zone #3, the setter (player #6) again must
be positioned behind and to the right of player #3 (Figure 3.6). The
path of the penetrating setter following the serve is in a lane also
to the right of player #3 but not so far over that player #2 will be
distracted. To ensure that no distractions occur, the penetrating
setter must make an effort to get to the net as quickly as possible
following the server's initial contact with the ball. In fact, following this rationale, the setter would also be acquiring more time to
become comfortably positioned in the frontcourt.

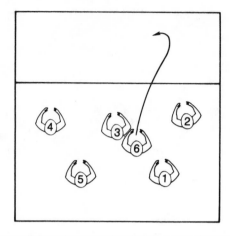

Figure 3.6 Player #6 penetrating to the frontcourt from zone #3.

Player #5 Penetrating From Zone #4

When penetrating from zone #4, the setter (player #5) is faced with two major difficulties. First, the setter must now run a much far-ther distance across the court before arriving in the setter's posi-tion. Second, the setter must move to that position without distracting the attention of the receiving players. Figure 3.7 illus-trates one possible solution for the penetrating setter. By lining up behind and to the left of player #4, player #5 would travel forward to the net and along its length to the setter's position. This method of penetration is not recommended. If penetrating along this route,

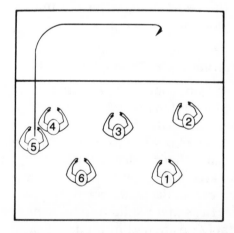

Figure 3.7 Player #5 penetrating to the frontcourt from zone #4.

the setter would in fact be increasing the distance that must be covered in order to arrive in the frontcourt setter's position. This would increase the length of time the setter would be in transit, which would decrease the possibility of the setter being properly positioned when the received serve had been passed to the frontcourt.

In order to avoid these difficulties, there are three possible alternatives for the receiving team.

The first alternative is to have the penetrating setter (player #5) begin in a position behind and to the right of player #4 (Figure 3.8). Immediately following the serve, the setter moves forward in a lane to the right of player #4 until a point just beyond the attack line. At this point, the setter begins to angle over directly to the setter's frontcourt position. During this movement, however, the setter must maintain eye contact with the served ball and the potential receiver.

When crossing the width of the court, it is very easy to lose sight of the served ball. Should this happen, the setter is immediately at a disadvantage from not knowing the origin of the first pass. At all times the penetrating setter must be aware of both the ball and the positioning of his or her teammates.

A second alternative is to have the setter penetrate to the front left side of the court. This effectively shortens the distance the setter must travel and decreases the possibility of distracting receiving players. There are many advantages and disadvantages when set-

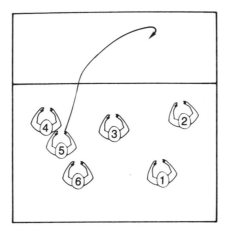

Figure 3.8 Player #5 penetrating along a somewhat shorter route from zone #4.

ting from the left side of the frontcourt. These will be described in greater detail in chapter 6.

The third solution is simply not to penetrate from zone #4. It may in fact be appropriate to have a frontcourt player set the ball. In most cases, a team will have two players on the court who are capable of setting the ball. These players are generally placed diametrically opposite one another on the court in order to ensure that on any given rotation, there is always a capable setter positioned in the frontcourt. Therefore, if you choose not to use the penetrating setter from zone #4, it may be prudent to utilize the front row setter in zone #2. The remaining discussion of the W serve reception formation will detail the various alternatives when using front row setters.

Frontcourt Setter From Zone #2

In some instances it may be prudent to make use of a frontcourt setter in lieu of a penetrating backcourt setter. One such instance occurs when a side out (winning back of the opponent's serve) is needed and your most talented setter is positioned in the frontcourt. In this situation, you may deem it most beneficial to have your premier setter directing the offense. However, there is a trade-off when choosing to use a frontcourt setter, the trade-off being that a three-hitter attack is no longer available with the frontcourt setter directing the offense. Although not optimal, the two-hitter attack can also be very effective when well planned and executed. Following are six potential options available when using a frontcourt setter who is positioned in zone #2.

Front Row Setter #2, With Eligible Hitters in Zones #3 and #4

Figure 3.9 depicts the positioning of player #2 in the frontcourt setter's position prior to the opposition's service of the ball. With this positioning it is unnecessary for player #5 to penetrate, which relieves many of the problems that have been discussed. The decision to use a frontcourt setter greatly diminishes the possibility of a weakened defense when receiving the opposition's serve. This improved defensive stability, however, can occur only at the expense of certain offensive possibilities.

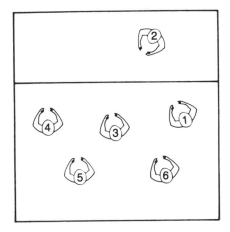

Figure 3.9   Front row setter in zone #2.

When penetrating a backcourt setter, there are three eligible hitters in the front row following reception of the serve. When using a front row player as a setter, one of the eligible hitters is effectively being eliminated. If player #2 is positioned at the net in the frontcourt setter's position, he or she must be replaced in the vacated receiving area by backcourt player #1. This is necessary to maintain the integrity of the W serve reception formation. However, as a backcourt player, player #1 is unable to act as a hitter in the frontcourt. The result is that following reception of the served ball, only two front row hitters remain eligible to attack. In Figure 3.9 the two eligible hitters are in zones #3 and #4. This ultimately diminishes several offensive possibilities by diminishing the area of concentration of the opposition's defense to that area occupied by the two eligible hitters.

Fake Penetration With Eligible Hitters in Zones #3 and #4

These negative effects can, however, be minimized. As illustrated in Figure 3.10, it appears that player #1 is in a position to penetrate to the frontcourt to set to the three-hitter attack. However, when the serve has been executed, it is player #2, not player #1, who moves up to the frontcourt setter's position. Player #1 remains in position to receive the serve should it be directed to that area. It is crucial that player #2 move ahead to the setter's position as soon as possible in order not to distract the attention of the now-receiving player #1. This is called *fake penetration*.

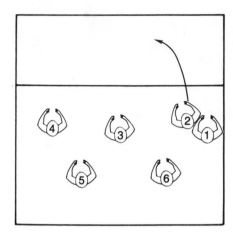

Figure 3.10   Player #1 fakes penetration allowing player #2 to move to the frontcourt setter's position.

The object of this fake penetration play is to make it appear to the defense that a setter will be penetrating, allowing a three-hitter attack. In actuality, though, the front row player, #2, moves to the frontcourt to set to a two-hitter attack. Although only two eligible hitters remain, the defense is under the impression that there are three eligible hitters, because they were exposed to a penetrating setter. This effectively spreads out the concentration of the defense to the three hitting positions rather than allowing the opposition to concentrate solely on the two eligible hitters. This is one very effective method of increasing the offensive advantage when using the front row setter and the resulting two-hitter attack.

Front Row Setter #2, With Eligible Hitters in Zones #2 and #3

Another method of increasing the offensive options, when using a front row player as setter, is to have eligible hitters in areas other than the conventional zones #3 and #4. Figure 3.11 demonstrates a situation where the two eligible hitters are positioned in zones #2 and #3. This now emphasizes an area of the defense that is not often exploited when the player in zone #2 is setting.

The only concern of the receiving team in this situation is that player #2 remain in the lane to the right of player #3 until the server contacts the ball. Should player #2 be in a lane to the left of player

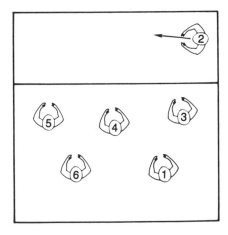

Figure 3.11 Front row setter #2 with eligible hitters in zones #2 and #3.

#3 before the serve, the player positioning of the serve reception formation would be illegal. It is the responsibility of player #2 to maintain the positional integrity of this serve reception formation.

Fake Penetration With Eligible Hitters in Zones #2 and #3

Figure 3.12 shows the positioning of players when faking penetration with eligible hitters in zones #2 and #3. In this instance, player #2 fakes penetration from behind player #3. Although player #2 is in fact a frontcourt player, it appears to the opposition that player #2 is penetrating from the backcourt. Again, this makes it appear to the opposition that the receiving team has three eligible hitters when there are in fact only two, diminishing the possibility of the defense concentrating on the two actual eligible hitters. Additionally, as in the previous case, player #2 must ensure that legal positioning is maintained by remaining in a position to the right of player #3 until the server contacts the ball.

Front Row Setter #2, With Eligible Hitters in Zones #2 and #4

A third possibility for front row setter positioning is illustrated in Figure 3.13. In this formation, eligible hitters are positioned in zones #2 and #4. This is offensively advantageous to the receiving team

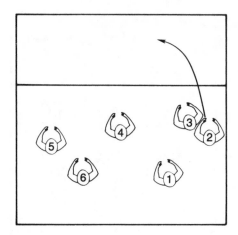

Figure 3.12   Player #2 faking penetration from behind player #3.

as it forces the middle blocker of the opposing team to concentrate on either end of the net rather than the much more convenient middle court area. As a result, the effectiveness of the middle defender hopefully is reduced.

As was the case with the previous formation, player #2 is responsible for maintaining the positional integrity of this serve reception formation by remaining in a lane to the right of player #3 until the server contacts the ball. Player #3 must also be certain to be

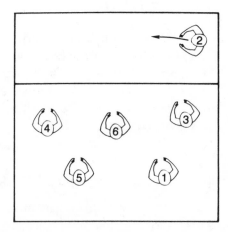

Figure 3.13   Player #2 in the frontcourt setting position with hitters in zones #2 and #4.

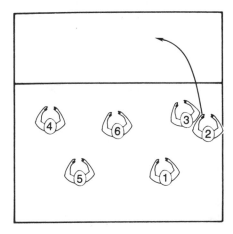

Figure 3.14 Player #2 fakes penetration with hitters in zones #2 and #4.

in a position ahead of player #6. Should player #3 move to a position laterally behind player #6, a positional fault would occur.

Fake Penetration With Eligible Hitters in Zones #2 and #4

The previous formation also lends itself to the possibility of fake penetration on the service reception. Once again, player #2 penetrates from behind player #3, creating the illusion of a three-hitter offense (Figure 3.14). In this instance again, only two eligible hitters are positioned in the frontcourt, yet the defense must be prepared to concentrate on all three front row players.

In this formation, the possibility for success favors the receiving team, as it places the defense at a disadvantage due to its perception of the receiving team's offensive capabilities. The only negative aspect of this formation lies in the possibility of players #3 and #6 overlapping, resulting in a positional fault. Player #6 must be sure to be behind player #3. Likewise, player #3 must be equally careful to maintain a position laterally ahead of player #6.

Frontcourt Setter From Zone #3

As was the case in the preceding section, there are many options available when using a frontcourt setter positioned in zone #3. Following are four examples of recommended positioning strategies.

Figure 3.15   Player #3 setting to eligible hitters in zones #2 and #4.

Front Row Setter #3, With Eligible Hitters in Zones #2 and #4

Figure 3.15 illustrates the positioning of players when front row player #3 acts as the setter. Backcourt player #6 moves forward to fill the void left by player #3 in the front row of serve receivers. In so doing, player #6 becomes a non-hitting front row player, leaving players #2 and #4 as the two remaining eligible hitters. These, however, are advantageous zones in which to have players positioned. Faced with hitters in zones #2 and #4, the defense must be prepared to defend either end of the net. This in turn will force the defense to spread out, limiting its ability to concentrate on any one specific zone.

In the frontcourt, player #3 must be careful not to move into the lane area to the right of player #2. Should this occur, an illegality in player positioning would result. Therefore, it is the responsibility of the setter (player #3) to maintain the positional integrity of the serve reception formation.

Fake Penetration With Eligible Hitters in Zones #2 and #4

As with previous fake penetrations, the object is to mislead the opposing players by having them believe that they must defend a three-hitter attack when in fact there are only two eligible hitters. Figure 3.16 diagrams the position of the two eligible hitters in zones #2 and #4 where the opposition must defend the entire length of the net. The setter (player #3) begins from a position in front of player #6 and moves to the frontcourt setter's position upon the

Figure 3.16 Player #3 faking penetration from zone #3 with eligible hitters in zones #2 and #4.

server's contact of the ball. This leaves player #6 available to receive any served ball directed into the area of responsibility of zone #3. The major positional responsibility of player #3 in this formation is to remain in a position ahead of player #6.

Front Row Setter #3,
With Eligible Hitters in Zones #2 and #3

Figure 3.17 shows the eligible hitters, #2 and #4, now located in zones #2 and #3. In some cases it may be advantageous to narrow the possible attack area. For instance, if the opposition in this

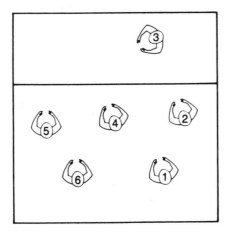

Figure 3.17 Player #3 setting to eligible hitters in zones #2 and #3.

rotation is weak in defending attacks from zones #2 and #3, it may be preferable to organize the hitters so that they are attacking this weakness. Regardless of the strategic logic, in this formation player #5 would be the nonhitting front row hitter, nullifying any outside attacks on the strong side.

The setter (player #3) is again responsible for maintaining the integrity of player positioning and must be careful not to overlap either player #2 or player #4. A further positional responsibility must be borne by players #4 and #5, who must be certain that they too do not overlap.

Fake Penetration With Eligible Hitters in Zones #2 and #3

Figures 3.18 and 3.19 each illustrate a distinctly different possibility for faking penetration when utilizing player #3 as the front row setter. In Figure 3.18 the setter, player #3, appears to be a serve receiver and player #2 the penetrating setter. In fact though, upon the server's contact of the ball player #3 vacates zone #3, leaving the responsibility for serve reception to player #2. In Figure 3.19 the setter (player #3) fakes penetration from behind player #4, leaving the receiving responsibilities for zone #3 in the hands of player #4.

In either case, only two eligible hitters remain, though the fake penetration should lead the opposition to believe that there is the possibility of a three-hitter attack. As was the case with the previ-

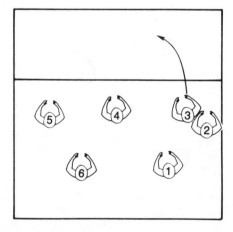

Figure 3.18 Player #3 faking penetration from zone #2 to set to eligible hitters in zones #2 and #3.

Figure 3.19 Player #3 penetrating from zone #3 to set to eligible hitters in zones #2 and #3.

ous serve reception formation, players #4 and #5 must be very careful to maintain their respective front and back row positioning. The importance of the positioning of players #4 and #5 should not, however, minimize the importance of the setter (player #3) maintaining lateral positioning when penetrating from either zone #2 or zone #3. As in all serve reception formations, the players must be very aware of their positioning in order to avoid careless positional faults.

Frontcourt Setter From Zone #4

Unlike the previous two instances where frontcourt setters originated in zones #2 and #3, there are few high quality, low risk positional arrangements when the frontcourt setter is positioned in zone #4. Following are two examples of the relatively few options available in this alignment.

Front Row Setter #4, With Eligible Hitters in Zones #2 and #3

When the front row setter originates in zone #4, player #5 must move forward to a receiving position in the front row (Figure 3.20). With player #5 in the front row as a nonhitting receiver, only players #2 and #3 remain as eligible hitters. When the front row setter (player #4) originates in this zone, the formation illustrated in Figure

3.20 is most often the only formation that can be implemented, other than to fake penetration. To attempt to relocate eligible hitters in any position other than zones #2 and #3 will force the setter (player #4) to begin from a position very close to the left sideline. This would ultimately cause the setter to move along the entire length of the net in order to get in setting position. As this is somewhat undesirable, the only standard positioning would be that illustrated in Figure 3.20.

In this instance, the positional responsibility for the setter is to remain in a position to the left of player #3 until the ball has been contacted by the server.

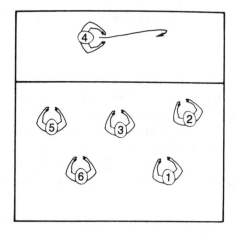

Figure 3.20   Player #4 setting to eligible hitters in zones #2 and #3.

Fake Penetration With Eligible Hitters in Zones #2 and #3

There is basically only one viable option for fake penetration in this formation also. This is to have the setter positioned in front of player #3, creating the illusion that player #3 is the setter penetrating to set a three-hitter attack (Figure 3.21). Again, however, following the server's contact with the ball, player #4 vacates zone #3. This leaves player #3 to receive the serve and, following that, to act as one of the two eligible hitters. Player #4 must be very cautious when faking penetration in this formation and must remain to the left of player #3. More importantly, he or she must be ahead of player #5 to avoid a positional fault.

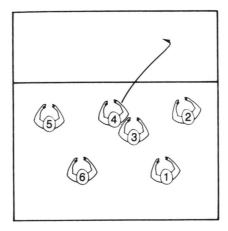

Figure 3.21 Player #4 faking penetration from zone #3 to set to eligible hitters in zones #2 and #3.

There are other positional possibilities with the front row setter originating in zone #4. Unfortunately, the advantages of these options for the most part do not exceed the high risks involved, and these options are therefore less desirable and not recommended.

Cup Serve Reception Formation

The cup formation has also been named for its appearance, as Figure 3.22 illustrates. At a glance, the most noticeable features of the cup formation are not only the fact that it resembles a cup but the fact that there are only four receiving players. As a result, this is a less defensive formation for service reception. Rather its emphasis is offense oriented.

In the cup formation, not only is the setter being hidden to avoid receiving the serve, but so is one of the eligible hitters. The effect of this is that once the ball has been received, there is a setter and at least one hitter who is in a position to execute a quick attack. As a result, strategic considerations notwithstanding, the decision to implement the cup formation will primarily depend upon the ability of the four receiving players. It is imperative that the receiving players be of a skill level higher than would be necessary to effect

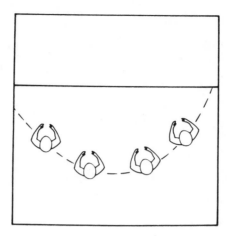

Figure 3.22 Basic positioning of four receiving players to form the cup effect of this serve reception formation.

the W serve reception formation. In light of this, the cup formation is used for the most part by more advanced teams who have a greater ability to consistently receive service.

Player Positioning

In the cup formation, it has been noted, both a setter and a hitter are hidden from the service, thus allowing them to prepare for a quick attack without the distraction of receiving the serve. To this end, the setter and hitter position themselves in an area of the frontcourt immediately behind the net where they are removed from the responsibility of receiving the serve.

Figure 3.23 illustrates the approximate positioning of the remaining four receiving players in relation to the prominent court boundaries. Players A and D position themselves approximately 3-6 feet from their respective sidelines. Although players A and D are in similar positions in relation to the attack line, player D is somewhat closer, being between 7 and 8 feet behind the attack line while player A is between 8 and 9 feet behind the attack line. As in the W serve reception formation, the positions of the players are not linear in relation to the baselines or attack lines. Instead, the focus and positioning of the players must be skewed somewhat so that the players are aligned with the opposition's service area.

Figure 3.23 also illustrates how the positioning of back row players B and C remains consistent with the premise applied to the positioning of players A and D. Player C is positioned in an area farther from the baseline (approximately 8-9 feet) and closer to the respective sideline (approximately 7-8 feet) than is player B, and player B is positioned approximately 7-8 feet inside the baseline and 8-9 feet from the left sideline. These approximate areas of player positioning are flexible, however, as they are directly related to the areas of responsibility of each receiving player. In situations where the responsibilities of the receiving players are altered, the positioning of those players should also be altered.

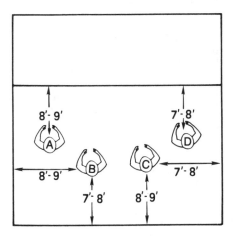

Figure 3.23 Positions of the four receiving players in relation to the prominent court boundaries.

Player Responsibilities

When receiving in the cup formation, players have straightforward responsibilities. Basically, the receiving court is divided into four approximately equal areas. These areas or lanes radiate from the server's position through the receiving court and to a point on the baseline of the receiving team. Figure 3.24 illustrates these four lanes in relation to the positioning of the four service receivers. In the most basic terms, all of these four players are responsible for receiving serves directed both in front of and behind their positions within their designated lane. As a result, the cup formation is much simpler than the W serve reception formation in terms of player responsibility. Whether the first pass is directed to a setter in the left or in the right frontcourt, the receiving responsibilities remain the same. However, as the receivers must be able to cover their lane from center line to baseline, all of the receivers must be very mobile and highly skilled passers.

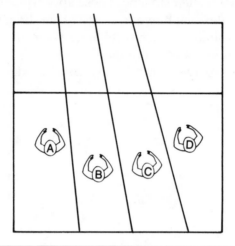

Figure 3.24 The four lanes of player responsibility when using the cup serve reception formation.

For the most part, the game situation responsibilities of the four receivers will vary. In certain situations, it may be necessary to have either player B or C cover the deep areas behind the respective players A and D. Likewise, it may also be prudent to have players A and D cover the shorter middle area ahead of the respective players B and C. As with the W serve reception formation, this is but a basic format for serve reception. Each formation can, and perhaps should, be positively developed into a formation of serve reception that will best address the specific needs of your team. These basic formations should serve as the basis for such alterations and adjustments.

Penetrating Setter With Designated Middle Hitter

When using a penetrating setter in the cup serve reception formation, it is possible to execute a three-hitter attack with the use of a designated middle hitter who is positioned to carry out a quick hit. (This type of hit will be more thoroughly covered in chapter 4.) There are a great number of combinations that allow any one of the frontcourt players to be positioned as the designated middle hitter and any one of the backcourt players as penetrating setter. It is the designated middle hitter who will be in a position to execute the quick attack. The designated middle hitter adds a new dimension to the already formidable three-hitter offense by providing a new offensive element—quickness. Following are a number of serve reception formations, involving various combinations of front- and backcourt players, that can best exploit the offensive potential of using a penetrating setter with the cup formation.

Player #1 Penetrating With Player #4 as Designated Middle Hitter

Figure 3.25 diagrams how player #4, the designated hitter, has been hidden behind the net near the left sideline. Player #4 is not in a position to receive the served ball; the reason for moving very near the left sideline is so that a positional overlap will not occur with player #3, who is in a position to receive the serve.

Player #1 (setter) begins in the area behind and to the right of player #2, again to avoid a positional overlap. In this position, player #1 moves to the frontcourt setter's position immediately following the server's contact of the ball.

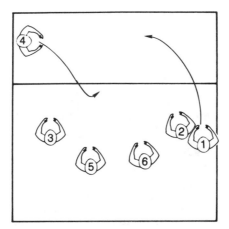

Figure 3.25 Player #1 penetrating while player #4 takes position behind the net in the cup serve reception formation.

At the same time, player #4 (designated hitter) moves to a position slightly behind the attack line in the middle court area. From here, player #4 can execute a quick hit approach through the middle hitter's area. The rationale for having the designated hitter move to the middle hitting area is to allow the quickest possible offensive attack. Were the designated hitter to attack from an outside hitter's position, valuable time would be consumed while the setter's pass traveled the additional distance to that position. Therefore, in an effort to minimize the possibility of a defensive block, it is essential that the designated hitter attack through the middle area. In so doing, he or she attacks from an area where the shortest pass and ultimately the quickest attack can be executed.

Following the first pass to the setter, the receiving team has a three-hitter attack. The designated hitter (player #4) attacks through the middle position, player #3 attacks from the strong outside position (the outside position that the setter is facing), and player #2 attacks from the weak outside position (the outside position behind the setter's field of vision). Should the quick attack through the middle not be possible, two eligible hitters still remain at either end of the net. This formation puts added pressure on the defense in that not only is there the planned possibility of a quick attack (planned by virtue of the cup formation itself) but there is also the need for the opposition to be prepared to defend offensive attacks at either end of the net. In many cases, the additional threat of having to defend two outside hitters will sufficiently slow down the reaction time of the middle blocker. This in turn will significantly advantage the three offensive hitters.

Player #1 Penetrating With Player #3 as Designated Middle Hitter

In this formation (Figure 3.26) player #1 (setter) again penetrates from behind player #2. Again, player #1 has the responsibility of being aware not to overlap the front row position of player #2 prior to the server's contact of the ball. In this formation, however, it is player #3 who has been given the responsibility of designated hitter. As such, player #3 takes a position behind the net where there are no serve reception responsibilities. In this frontcourt position, player #3 must remain in a lane to the right of player #4 so as not to overlap, causing a positional fault. As in the previous case, the designated hitter (player #3) leaves the sanctuary of the

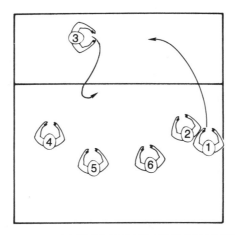

Figure 3.26 Player #1 penetrating to set to the three-hitter attack with player #3 as designated hitter.

net area as soon as the ball has been contacted by the server. Once again, the hitter moves behind the attack line in the middle area to approach for a quick attack in the middle position.

This formation also allows for a three-hitter attack with secondary hitters in both of the outside hitting positions. Player #4 would be the strong outside hitter, whereas player #2 would attack from the weak outside position. This three-hitter attack affords all of the offensive possibilities described in the previous serve reception formation, with the further advantage of player #3 beginning from a position much nearer to the ultimate middle attack position. This effectively minimizes the possibility of player #3 being late for the quick middle attack.

Player #1 Penetrating With Player #2 as Designated Middle Hitter

Figure 3.27 illustrates the formation of players when player #1 is penetrating and player #2 is the designated hitter. The initial positioning of players in this formation is considerably different from the positionings in the two previous serve reception formations in which player #1 penetrates to set.

The setter (player #1), could again penetrate from behind the player on the far right side of the receiving cup, in this case player #3. However, as player #2 is the designated hitter and hidden

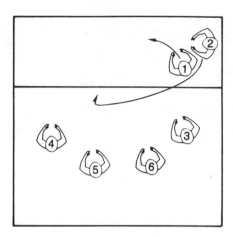

Figure 3.27 Player #1 penetrating with player #2 as designated hitter.

behind the net, player #1 can move forward to the frontcourt, yet remain behind player #2 to maintain positional integrity. It is preferred that player #1 penetrate from this frontcourt area, as this allows player #1 to attain a position much closer to the setter's position. This, consequently, limits the time and energy the penetrating setter must expend in order to move into the desired frontcourt setter's position. Additionally, player #1 must be aware not to begin in a position to the left of that diagramed in Figure 3.27. To do so may result in player #1 overlapping positionally with player #6.

Player #2 (designated hitter) is positioned close to the net, again in order not to be involved in serve reception, yet very close to the right sideline. This is necessary in order not to overlap positionally with the receiving player #3. In this formation, as in all serve reception formations, the players must be very conscious of their initial positions so that they avoid careless positional faults.

Following the serve, player #1 moves left to the frontcourt setter's position, while player #2 moves to the initial attacking area in the middle hitter's position. Again, a three-hitter attack is possible, with player #4 attacking from the strong outside position and player #3 attacking from the weak outside position.

Player #6 Penetrating With Player #3 as Designated Middle Hitter

When using player #6 as the penetrating setter, there is but one formation possibility (Figure 3.28). To use any other formation

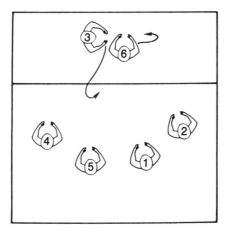

Figure 3.28 Player #6 penetrating to set the three-hitter attack with player #3 as designated hitter.

would either remove the setter and designated hitter from the front-court or would result in positional faults prior to the service. Therefore, as illustrated in Figure 3.28, both player #3 (designated hitter) and player #6 (penetrating setter) begin from initial positions in the middle front court area. Player #6 must be aware not to move ahead of front row player #3 and must be careful to remain positioned laterally between back row players #5 and #1 until the server has contacted the ball.

Once the server has contacted the ball, player #6 (setter) moves to the frontcourt setter's position while player #3 (designated hitter) moves to a position slightly behind the attack line in the middle court area. From here a quick middle attack is executed. Again, using a penetrating back row setter there is the possibility of a three-hitter attack. Should the quick middle attack not be possible, player #4 is available to attack from the strong outside position along with player #2, who would attack from the weak outside position.

Player #5 Penetrating With Player #4 as Designated Middle Hitter

As in the previous case when player #6 penetrates to the front court, there is only one formation possible when player #5 is the penetrating setter. Figure 3.29 shows the positioning of players when player #5 penetrates and player #4 acts as the designated hitter. Both players #4 (designated hitter) and #5 (penetrating setter) initially

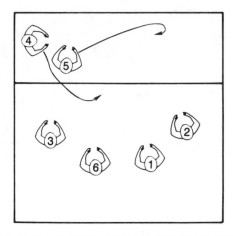

Figure 3.29   Positioning of players when player #5 penetrates to set with player #4 as designated hitter.

are positioned in the frontcourt in an area very close to the left sideline. In fact, player #4 must be in a position extremely close to the sideline in order to avoid a lateral positional fault with player #3, who would be among the four players receiving the service. Player #5 also must be close to the sideline in order to remain laterally outside player #6. An additional responsibility for player #5 is to remain behind player #4, again to retain the positional integrity of the serve reception formation.

Following the server's contact of the ball, the responsibilities of the setter (player #5) and the designated hitter (player #4) are the same as were required in the previous formations. Player #5 moves to the frontcourt setter's position and player #4 moves to an area behind the attack line in the middle court area in preparation for a quick middle attack. Again, the penetrating setter affords the luxury of a three-hitter attack with player #3 in the strong outside position and player #2 in the weak outside position.

Front Row Setter With Designated Middle Hitter

As was the case in the W serve reception formation, there are certain instances in the cup serve reception formation when it may be prudent to use a frontcourt setter to direct the offense. This may be a result of outstanding passing skills possessed by the frontcourt setter, familiarity of front row setter and designated middle hitter, or simply skill level of the players involved. Whatever the reasons for using a frontcourt setter, the options and available patterns of play with only two hitters are still very much unlimited. Though one of the available frontcourt hitters is eliminated, many other possible advantages arise through fakes and deceptive alignments. Some of these possible alignments will be detailed now.

Player #4 Setting With Player #3 as Designated Middle Hitter

Figure 3.30 illustrates a formation in which a front row player (#4) is used as a setter rather than as a backcourt player. This situation most often arises if a team has only one skilled setter and must therefore forego a three-hitter attack in an effort to ensure a well-set ball following the serve reception. By either necessity or strategic design, this formation, and those that follow, allows only a two-hitter attack. As a result, should the quick middle attack not be possible, only one eligible hitter would remain. The defense would then have the advantage of concentrating their efforts on two rather than three possible areas of attack. Perhaps one positive possibility for the receiving team in this formation is that the setter can now execute a quick second hit on a pass from the backcourt. As the setter is now a front row player, this attack would be legal. This in itself is not a dramatic offensive weapon but may

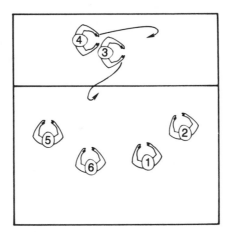

Figure 3.30 Front row setter #4 setting a two-hitter attack with player #3 as designated hitter.

be useful to teams with setters who are capable of consistently hitting the ball. At the very least this offers a unique offensive possibility that may be used successfully by the receiving team.

As illustrated in Figure 3.30 both player #4 (setter) and player #3 (designated hitter) begin in positions in the middle of the frontcourt. In this formation, the responsibility for player positioning is relatively simple in that players #4 and #3 must only be aware not to laterally overlap. Following the service, player #4 moves directly to the frontcourt setter's position as player #3 moves to the middle hitter's position. This leaves only player #2 to attack from the weak outside position. Accordingly, the opposition can concentrate their defensive efforts on attacks coming only from zones #2 and #3.

It is possible, however, to fake a three-hitter attack. This is easily done by having player #5 move to the middle attack area following the serve. From here player #5 attacks through the middle area and fakes a quick middle hit. Player #3, rather than moving to the middle area, moves to the strong outside position. The ultimate effect of this formation is to place eligible hitters at either end of the net while faking a quick middle attack. In many instances, the illusion of a three-hitter attack can be just as effective as actually having a three-hitter attack. To be successful, however, the fake middle hitter (player #5) must be convincing enough to immobilize the opposition's middle blocker. Once the middle blocker has committed himself or herself to defending the quick middle attack, the outside hitters have a clear advantage when hitting against a one-player block. In this situation, the ultimate effect of the two-hitter attack is much the same as were a three-hitter attack to have been implemented.

Player #4 Setting With Player #2 as Designated Middle Hitter

Figure 3.31 depicts the only other formation possible when player #4 acts as the setter. This formation is somewhat undesirable due to the distance player #4 must travel before arriving in the setter's position. However, it may be worth the risk in that both eligible hitters are now on the strong side of the court. It may in fact be necessary to take the risks inherent in this formation, should player #3 be physically or psychologically unable to execute a quick middle attack.

These considerations notwithstanding, player #4 (setter) must be-

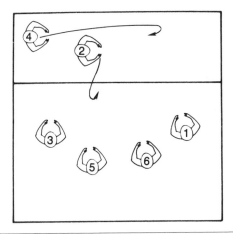

Figure 3.31 Player #4 setting to player #2 as designated hitter.

gin from a position to the extreme left of the frontcourt. Were player #4 to move a significant distance from the left sideline, it would almost surely cause a lateral overlap with player #3. Player #2 (designated hitter) may begin from a position in the frontcourt anywhere to the right of player #3. However, it is recommended that player #2 begin in a position as close to the middle as possible. This shortens the distance player #2 must travel to prepare for the quick middle attack. At the same time as player #2 moves into position behind the attack line, player #4 moves to the frontcourt setter's position.

In this formation the only eligible hitter other than player #2 is player #3 in the strong outside hitter's position. Once again all of the disadvantages of a two-hitter attack apply. A further inadequacy of this formation is that it is not possible to use a back row player as a fake quick middle hitter. Therefore, this truly is a two-hitter attack.

Player #3 Setting With Player #4 as Designated Middle Hitter

Figure 3.32 diagrams the positioning of both the setter (player #3) and the designated hitter (player #4) in this serve reception formation. Player #3 takes position immediately in the area of the frontcourt setter. Meanwhile, player #4 begins in a frontcourt position near the middle of the court. From here, player #4 has a very short distance to travel to arrive at the preattack position in the middle of the court, slightly behind the attack line.

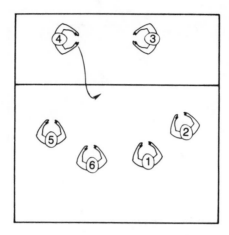

Figure 3.32   Player #3 setting to the two-hitter attack with player #4 as designated hitter.

As can be imagined, this would be an excellent formation if the goal were to minimize the movement of players. Unfortunately, this formation allows only a two-hitter attack, as the only other eligible hitter is player #2 in the weak outside position. It is possible, however, to fake a three-hitter attack by having player #5 fake the quick middle hit and having player #4 move back to the strong outside position. Implementing this alternative would cause the defense to spread out, as eligible hitters would now be positioned in both of the outside hitting areas. Again in this situation, the more convincing the illusion of a three-hitter attack, the greater the likelihood for success.

Player #3 Setting With Player #2 as Designated Middle Hitter

Figure 3.33 depicts the positioning of players when player #3 acts as the setter and player #2 acts as the designated hitter. In this formation, as in the previous one, the setter (player #3) may take position immediately in the frontcourt setter's position, eliminating the need to move at any time other than to retrieve a misdirected first pass following serve reception. The designated hitter (player #2) would begin in a frontcourt position to the right of player #3. This is necessary to maintain the lateral positioning of both players #2 and #3.

Following the server's contact of the ball, player #2 moves directly to a position somewhat behind the attack line in the middle court area and executes a quick middle attack. Once player #2 has com-

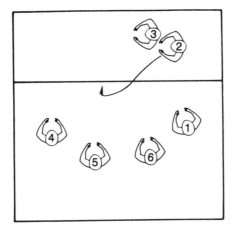

Figure 3.33   Positioning of players with player #3 setting and player #2 as designated hitter.

mitted this quick attack, only one other eligible hitter remains: Player #4 is available in the strong outside hitter's position should the setter be unable or unprepared to execute a quick middle hit to player #2.

Player #2 Setting With Player #3 as Designated Middle Hitter

The formation diagramed in Figure 3.34 represents a situation in which, again, minimal movement of the setter and designated hitter

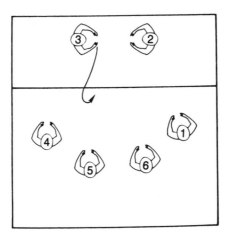

Figure 3.34   Player #2 setting with player #3 as designated hitter in this cup serve reception formation.

is required. In fact, the setter (player #2) is not required to move at all from the initial position in the frontcourt setter's area. The designated hitter (player #3) has only to move behind the attack line to arrive in preattack position. Once in this position, player #3 can execute a quick middle attack.

The secondary hitter in this formation is player #4 in the strong outside hitter's position. Unfortunately, whenever player #2 acts as the front row setter, it is impossible to have a back row player positioned to fake a quick middle attack. Therefore, it is necessary to effect the illusion of a three-hitter attack by other means.

Player #2 Faking Penetration With Player #3 as Designated Middle Hitter

Figure 3.35 illustrates one formation that may be used in order to create the illusion of a three-hitter attack. As in the previous formation, player #3 (designated hitter) is positioned in the middle of the frontcourt area prior to the server's contact of the ball. Player #2 (setter), however, begins in a position slightly ahead of player #1. In this alignment, it appears that player #1 is preparing to penetrate in order to set to a three-hitter attack. This is not the case, however. At the time of the serve, it is player #2 rather than player #1 who moves forward to the frontcourt setter's position. Player #1 instead remains as one of the four service receivers.

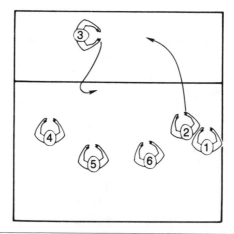

Figure 3.35 Player #2 faking penetration with player #3 as designated hitter causing the illusion of a three-hitter attack.

Although there are in fact only two eligible hitters, located in zones #3 and #4, the defense will be under the assumption that they must defend three eligible hitters. The result of this is that the defense will be unable to concentrate solely on the two eligible hitters. Instead, the opposition must spread out in preparation to defend the entire length of the net. This gives a considerable offensive advantage to the receiving team.

Player #2 Setting With Player #4 as Designated Middle Hitter

Figure 3.36 diagrams the second of two possible formations resulting in a purely two-hitter attack when using player #2 as the front row setter. In this instance, player #2 (setter) again remains in the initial position of the frontcourt setter. Player #4 (designated hitter) begins in a position very close to the left sideline. This is necessary to avoid lateral overlapping with receiving player #3. Following the serve, player #4 moves to the preattack area in the middle court area behind the attack line. While player #4 is executing the quick middle attack, player #3 is prepared to attack from the strong outside hitter's position. This again is a formation that results in only a basic two-hitter attack. There is also, however, the possibility of disguising this two-hitter attack as a three-hitter attack.

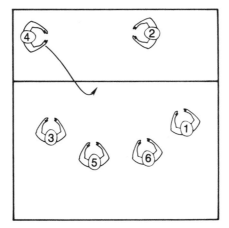

Figure 3.36 Player #2 setting with player #4 as designated hitter.

Player #2 Faking Penetration With Player #4
as Designated Middle Hitter

The premise of this formation is identical to that of the formation where player #2 is the setter and player #3 is the designated hitter (refer to Figure 3.35). In Figure 3.37 the position and direction of player movement is illustrated. Player #4 (designated hitter) begins from an initial position very close to the left sideline, again to avoid a positional fault with player #3. Player #2 (setter) begins in a position slightly ahead of player #1, making it appear as though player #1 is penetrating to set to a three-hitter attack. When the ball has been contacted by the server, it is player #2 rather than player #1 who vacates the receiving area. Player #1 remains in the cup formation to receive the service. Player #2 moves forward to the front-court setter's area to set to either the quick middle attack of player #4 or to the strong outside hitter, player #3.

Although this is in fact only a two-hitter attack, the opposition will react to the illusion of a penetrating setter and believe that a three-hitter attack is possible. As before, this will spread out the defense and prohibit a concentrated defensive effort in the areas of the two actual eligible hitters. This advantages the receiving team by allowing them to execute a two-hitter attack with almost all of the possibilities of a three-hitter attack. The only disadvantage is that the setter will in fact have only two eligible hitters to whom he or she may set the ball.

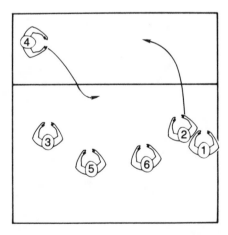

Figure 3.37 Player #2 faking penetration with player #4 as designated hitter.

It has been illustrated throughout this chapter that the essence of serve reception is deception. The responsibility of the coach extends far beyond simply teaching the skills of serve reception. The coach must also be prepared to teach the strategies and inherent tactics of serve reception. Only then can the players effectively put to use the skills they have been taught. It is ultimately essential that all players have a complete understanding of the strategies involved in serve reception, if they are to effectively fulfill their roles and responsibilities within the team concept.

Chapter 4

Offense

Following reception of the serve or after successfully defending an opponent's attack, your team will find itself in an offensive situation. The premise of the basic offense is that no more than three contacts shall be used in order to set up an attack against your opponent. In most cases, teams will opt to use the full three contacts unless the situation will not allow it. When using three contacts, the first pass following serve reception is directed to the setter. Therefore, this will be the first area of consideration.

The First Pass

The first pass is directed to the frontcourt area so that it may be played by the setter. From this frontcourt position, the setter may execute a second pass to any one of the available frontcourt attackers. It is very important, however, that the first pass be an accurate one. The more accurate the pass to the setter, the more able the setter will be to make a good set. In light of the importance of the first pass to the ultimate success of the overall offensive attack, a number of considerations should be addressed.

Following are a number of considerations and guidelines that should be examined when developing any offensive strategy.

Setting Areas

There are basically three areas in which the setter may receive the first pass. They are (A) the middle, (B) the right, and (C) the left (Figure 4.1). These are three choices for where the offensive set (second hit) may take place, each having its own merit.

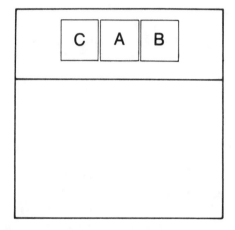

Figure 4.1   The three areas to which the first pass may be directed.

Pass to the Middle

The decision to pass to the middle should generally be reserved for those teams using a two-hitter offense. By passing to the middle, the setter may pass to either sideline (Figure 4.2). Having a hitter on each side of the court forces the defense to spread out. This can give your hitters an advantage because the defense must be prepared to defend attacks from either sideline.

Although this situation is favorable for the spikers, it is not quite so favorable for the setter. If the setter chooses to face the hitter to whom he or she is setting, the defense will key in on that hitter. The only option for the setter is to consistently face one or the other sideline. This allows the setter to pass forward only to one hitter while having to backset to the other. To be able to use both hitters,

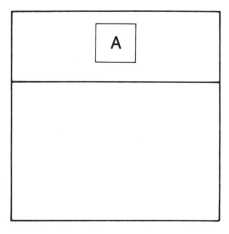

Figure 4.2 The middle setting area.

the setter must be able to consistently execute the more difficult backset. The difficulty of the backset will be magnified if the setter is young or inexperienced.

Passing to the middle is not advisable for teams using a three-hitter offense. The major disadvantage is that with the setter occupying the middle area, you will effectively be erasing the use of your middle hitter on offense. A three-hitter system is best suited to passes either on the left or right of the middle set position.

Pass to the Right

This is the area most often passed to by teams using both the two- and three-hitter offenses. By setting from an area closer to the sideline, the setter has a better view of the defensive and offensive court area (Figure 4.3). Setting from the right of middle also favors right-handed (or onside) hitters because the ball is passed into their right spiking hand. This is preferred because it allows the spiker to compensate for poorly passed sets.

The three-hitter offense offers the further advantage of the setter's now being able to execute a forward pass to two hitters (left outside and middle) while backsetting to a third (right outside). Because the forward pass is generally preferred to the backset for its reliability, this is a positive advantage. The backset is now more reliable also, because the pass will travel over a shorter distance than if set from the middle area.

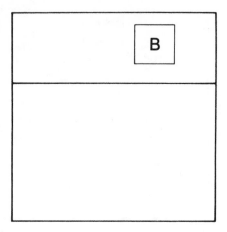

Figure 4.3   The setting area right of the middle.

With a two-hitter system you can also benefit by placing both hitters to the left of the setter. Here again all hitters receive more reliable forward-passed sets. The imminent trade-off is that the defense can now assume that the attack will come from the left half of the offensive court.

Passing the ball to the right set position also has merit when considering the ease with which your team can make the transition from defense to offense. The greater percentage of attacks are from the opponent's left side of the court (opponent's zones #2 and #3). An even higher percentage of these attacks are in the form of cross-court spikes that, hit diagonally across the court, end in your left side of the court (zones #5 and #6). As it is easier to return a pass in the same direction from which the ball is received, it is logical that the setter be placed in a position forward and to the right of the defensive digger (Figure 4.4). This allows the first pass to be made diagonally back in the same direction to the setter without any unnecessary change in positioning.

Pass to the Left

Offensively, passing to this area is preferred by teams with a majority of left-handed hitters (Figure 4.5). With the set coming from the left to the right side of the court, left-handed hitters are now the onside hitters (receiving the ball from the same side as their spiking arm). An advantage here is that defenses generally do not expect a strong attack from the right side (zones #2 and #3) of the offensive court.

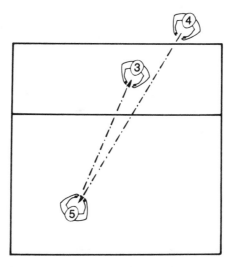

Figure 4.4 This demonstrates the assumption that the ball can more easily be returned in the direction from which it is received.

Defensively, there is the disadvantage that the cross-court spike must be returned at a refractory angle to the left middle passing area. As the crosscourt spike from the opponent's left side (zones #3 and #4 of opponent's court) is the most common, this will disadvantage the digger, who must pass forward and to the left of center (Figure 4.6). Perhaps it is because the pass to the left appears to have negligible advantages that few teams endeavor to set from the left frontcourt area. Just as most teams favor the more

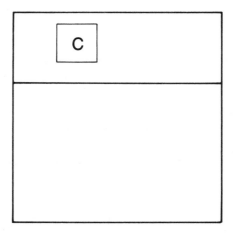

Figure 4.5 The left setting area.

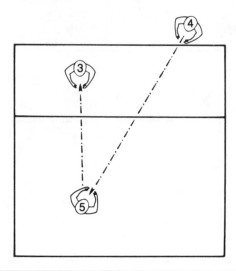

Figure 4.6 The refractory angle at which the received ball must now be returned.

advanced three-hitter attack, so most teams favor the pass to the right set position.

In order to simplify the discussions of the remaining chapters, all offensive systems shall be based on the premise that the desired pass is to the right set position. By simply reversing the conditions, you may also apply the information to passes directed to the left set position.

Position and Movement of the Setter

Immediately prior to reception of the ball, the setter should be moving toward the right set position approximately 2-5 feet away from the net (Figure 4.7). The setter should be in a ready position facing the left sideline. This is preferred to the position in which the setter's back is to the net, as facing the sideline increases the setter's ability to see the defensive court area. When open to the entire court, the setter is not only able to watch his or her own team preparing to attack but can also watch the defensive reactions of the opponent.

It is additionally important that, when approaching the net, the setter does not enter the area into which the first pass preferably should be directed (Figure 4.7). The setter should instead wait behind this area and move into it only when the ball is in flight to

Figure 4.7 The position of the setter behind the right setting area prior to the first pass.

that area. In this way, the setter will be moving forward into the ball. The advantages of this positioning are several: The setter will have a wider field of vision, the forward momentum of the setter can be redirected upward to ensure a strong set, and it is ensured that the setter is not in a stationary position. This gives the setter a jump on any misdirected passes.

Position and Movement of the Hitters

While the first pass is en route to the setter, the frontcourt hitters should be moving parallel to the net to positions from which they will begin their hitting approaches (Figure 4.8). When the setter receives the ball, the hitters should be angling toward the net in preparation for their final approach and take off (Figure 4.9). Dependent upon what type of set is expected, the angle and speed of approach may vary for each hitter. Nevertheless, Figure 4.9 accurately illustrates the pattern of approach for the majority of sets.

Basic Offensive Attacks

There are two major offensive attacks: the two-hitter attack and the three-hitter attack. The two-hitter attack incorporates two frontcourt players in the hitting role while the third frontcourt player

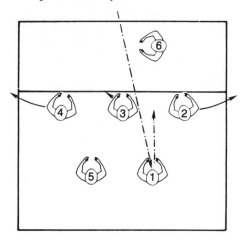

Figure 4.8 The lateral movement of the hitters while the first pass is en route to the setter.

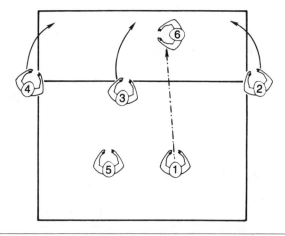

Figure 4.9 The forward movement of the hitters as they anticipate the set.

sets. The setter may be either the middle player or one of the outside players in the frontcourt.

The three-hitter attack uses all three frontcourt players as hitters and uses one of the backcourt players as the setter. The penetrating backcourt setter can again come from either the middle or one of the outside backcourt positions.

Two-Hitter Attack With #3 Setting

This system is used by teams employing a 6-0 or 3-3 offense and by some teams using a 4-2 offense (Figure 4.10). (These numerical

Figure 4.10   Two-hitter attack with the #3 player setting.

offensive systems will be discussed in greater detail later in this chapter.) Having hitters at each sideline forces the defense to spread out and be ready for a full shift of focus depending upon where the attack comes from. The middle blocker of the defense must now also be prepared to cover the entire length of the net in order to execute a double block with his or her front row counterparts. This system should afford many opportunities for the hitters to face only a one-player block.

Two-Hitter Attack With #2 Setting

This system is used by most teams employing a 6-0, 3-3, or 4-2 offensive system and teams using a 5-1 offense when the setter has

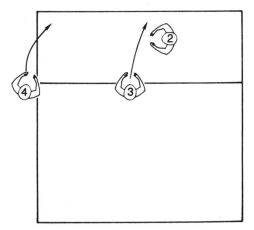

Figure 4.11   Two-hitter attack with the #2 player setting.

rotated to the frontcourt and is in, or has switched to, the #2 (right front) position (Figure 4.11). The advantage of this system is that if #3 and #4 are right-handed you have two onside hitters receiving forward passed sets. This system of attack also gives you the added advantage of being able to use quick sets to the middle hitter. The improvement is that you now have two speeds for your offense: the slower speed of the high sets (outside) and the much quicker speed of the sets to the middle. What the defense gains in knowing that your offensive attack is coming from only half the court, they will lose in not knowing how quickly it will come.

Three-Hitter Attack With Penetrating Setter

This attack is used by teams employing the 5-1 system when the setter is in the backcourt (Figure 4.12). It is also used by teams employing the 2-2-2 and 4-2 systems when and if they choose to have the setter penetrate. The penetration by the setter is most easily executed during serve reception or a free ball situation. However, the 5-1 system generally requires that it be carried out on almost every play.

This system allows all three of the front row players to attack offensively. You will have the two onside hitters of the two-hitter attack, with the extra advantage of a third offside hitter. Thus your offense extends along the entire length of the net.

To deal with this situation, the defense must spread out and be prepared to defend against spikes from three general areas. The

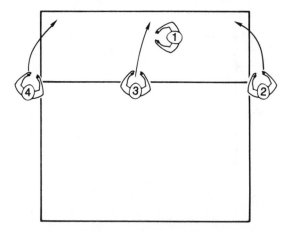

Figure 4.12   Three-hitter attack with a backcourt penetrating setter.

positive result, from an offensive point of view, is that your hitters will likely face only a single block or a late double block. This, along with the ability to change the speed of the offense, will give you virtually unlimited offensive options. There are also countless variations if your team can execute multiple offenses from the three-hitter attack. It should be apparent, however, that only teams of solid skill and experience should use the more complicated systems of attack. It is the responsibility of the coach to determine what level of difficulty his or her team is capable of mastering.

Offensive Sets—The High Sets

The following section deals with various types of offensive sets that can be used with both the two-hitter attacks and the three-hitter attack. Each type of set is discussed in order, from the basic to the more complex sets.

High Outside Set

As the name implies, this is a high arching set (at least 6-8 feet) directed to either the left or the right sideline area. The ball should extend out almost to the sideline antennas so that, if it were untouched, it would land outside the court area (Figure 4.13). The ball should be set approximately 1-3 feet back from the net, allowing the hitter a comfortable margin in which to contact the ball.

This set is useful for spreading out the defense, as it draws the blockers out to the sideline of the court. This allows the hitter the possibility of an easy wipe-off hit against the block. The remaining defenders must also be aware of the additional angles of attack open now that the hitter is hitting from virtually outside the court. The #4 outside hitter, by being outside the court, can now make a longer crosscourt spike than when closer to the center of the court. This will prove advantageous to shorter hitters or those with slow, flat spikes. The defense must also be aware of the possibility of a line spike. This spike is now more easily accomplished because the hitter does not have to use as much upper body rotation to put a spike close to the line. When hitting from a position closer to the center, the onside hitter must rotate his or her upper body a great deal in order to execute a line spike. As a result, this feat is rarely accomplished by the average hitter.

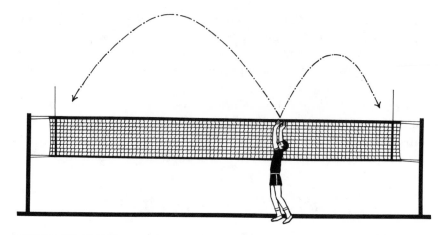

Figure 4.13 Demonstrates the path of the high outside set. The arrows designate the hitter's point of contact.

The advantages of the high outside set can easily be erased, however, if the setter fails to set the ball in the required area. Sets that are 3-5 feet inside the sideline will prove to be disastrous. Such sets are slow and must be very wide in order to compensate for their slowness. It is imperative that the setter give the hitter the advantage of improved angles of attack, especially with such a slow type of set. Setters must be consistent with this pass.

High Inside Set

This set is much the same as the high outside set with the exception that the hitter is attacking from the middle position (Figure 4.14). Again the set should be approximately 1-3 feet off the net and at least as high as the outside sets. The exact location along the net at which the ball should be set varies with circumstance. In a middle hitting situation, the setter and hitter must work more closely together than is necessary in an outside hitting situation. As a result, the hitter must be prepared to adjust according to the positioning of the setter. The formula for maintaining the desired setter-hitter relationship is as follows:

The hitter must move a distance away from the setter equal to the distance of the setter from the net.

Figure 4.15 depicts the ideal setter-hitter relationship for the high middle set. Unfortunately, the setter will not always receive a pass

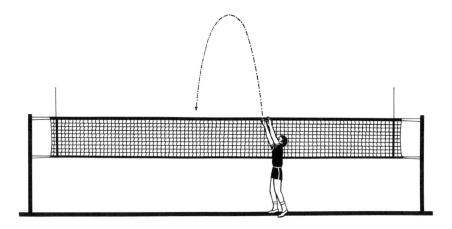

Figure 4.14 Demonstrates the path of the high inside set. The arrows designate the hitter's point of contact.

1-3 feet off the net. Therefore, the farther off the net the setter receives the ball, the farther down the net the hitter should attack the set (Figure 4.16). In all cases, the distance of setter to net and hitter to setter should be the same.

There will also be occasions when the setter will receive a pass 1-3 feet off the net but out of position along the length of the net. If the setter receives a pass in the center or to the *right* of center

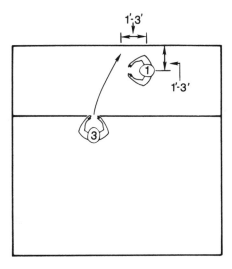

Figure 4.15 The setter passes the ball to a point equal to his or her distance from the net.

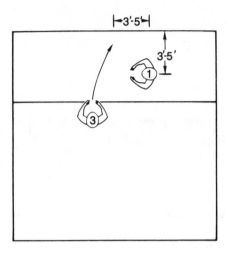

Figure 4.16 The farther the setter moves away from the net, the farther along the net he or she will set the ball.

along the net, the hitter must also move along the net to maintain the appropriate relationship (Figure 4.17). If, as in Figure 4.18, the setter must retrieve a pass along the net to the *left* of center, the hitter moves behind rather than in front of the setter to contact the ball. The relationship is maintained in a reverse order and executed with a back set. It is not advisable to have the hitter attempt to attack on the setter's left side in this situation for two reasons. First, the hitter would then be in a position in which a normal hitting

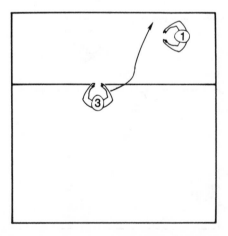

Figure 4.17 Hitter's path of attack when the setter is passing from the extreme right.

Figure 4.18   Hitter's path of attack when the setter is passing from the left of center.

approach on the net is not possible. He or she would instead have to approach from behind the setter and move in a direction away from the setter in order to make contact with the set ball. This is not an enviable approach from which to hit, especially for a right-handed hitter. The second reason is that hitting to the left of the setter may create confusion between the middle and outside hitters. With less skilled or inexperienced players, this possibility may become a probability.

Offensive Sets—The Quick Sets

Quick sets are passes designed to catch the defense unprepared and out of position. This contrasts sharply with the slower high sets, which were designed to spread out the defense and increase the angles of attack. Simply stated, quick sets are exactly that: sets executed quickly before the defense has the opportunity to react. The basic premise of the quick set is that *if the time between setter contact and hitter contact is decreased, the ability of the defense to respond appropriately to the situation will also be decreased.*

When the quick set is employed as part of the offense, the defense begins to "key" on hitters at the expense of watching the setter or the set. Accordingly, the blocking suffers, as each blocker is preoccupied with stopping the opposite attacker from scoring a quick set hit. This increases the probability of creating the ideal situation. It becomes very likely that your hitters will isolate the defense and create a one-player block situation, which highly favors the offensive hitter.

The quick set can also work very effectively to the overall team advantage. If properly applied, the quick set can act as a set-up for the high sets and vice versa. It seems clear that the ability of a team to master both the high and quick sets will be directly proportional to that team's ability to manipulate the opposition.

These results, however, can be expected only if the setters and hitters are able to execute a coordinated effort. It is imperative that the setter consistently deliver the ball to the correct area. With the increased speed of the sets, the margin for error is greatly diminished. It is the responsibility of the setter to consistently deliver the ball to the hitter. This type of set is unique in that it is the hitter rather than the setter who sets the pace for the attack. Since the hitter has begun the approach on the net before the setter has the ball, the setter must be ready to quickly and accurately deliver the ball to the hitter. It is therefore very important that the setter be given ample opportunity to practice quick setting to all hitters. More experienced players tend to delay the approach time, and younger players tend to speed it up. The result is that the setter will have to adjust his or her passes to complement each individual hitter. This can be successfully achieved only through the familiarization repeated practice brings.

Outside Shoot

Here it is the setter's objective to pass a quick set that drops from its flat trajectory to a point 1 foot above the net in front of the outside (#4) hitter (Figure 4.19). The ball should at no time travel more than 2 feet above the net, as any increased arc will slow down the flight time of the pass. When the passed ball has reached the setter's hands, the hitter should already have begun approach and be approximately 6-8 feet in back of the point where he or she should contact the ball (Figure 4.20).

If the setter and hitter both execute properly, the hitter should be facing a single block or no block at all. It is unlikely that the opposing middle blocker would be able to react and move in time to complete the double block outside. As a result the hitter should

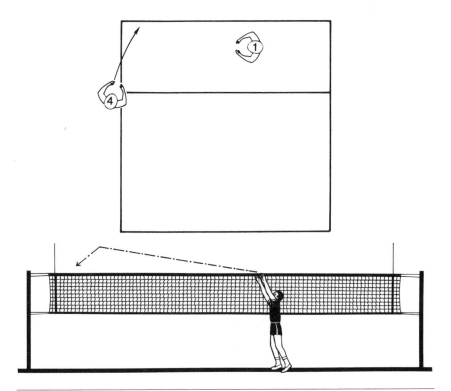

Figure 4.19 The outside shoot set illustrating the flight of the ball and the path of the attacker's movement.

Figure 4.20 Illustrates the timing of the hitter's approach for the outside shoot. The hitter should be approximately 6-8 feet from the point of contact when the ball is in the setter's hands.

see a gap between the outside (#2) and middle (#3) blockers through which he or she can hit crosscourt. In the event that the backcourt diggers shift around to protect the crosscourt attack, the hitter may spike down the line where only one digger (#1) behind the block is prepared to defend.

The effect of this type of attack is very telling on the defense. The middle blocker may become anxious to provide a double block; thus a fake outside shoot would open up the middle zone. The outside blocker may be determined to stick with the outside hitter and not ready to assist in middle blocking, giving the middle hitter the opportunity to hit a cut back between the open block.

Inside Shoot

For the setter, the inside shoot resembles the outside shoot in almost every respect. The only difference is that this set is made to a contact point approximately 6-8 feet inside the left sideline (Figure 4.21). With this set, the outside (#4) hitter approaches an area of attack such that he or she will be spiking between the middle (#3) and outside (#2) blockers. In the outside shoot, the pass was made to a point in front of the outside blocker. With the inside shoot, the pass is closer to the center of the court, forcing both the outside and middle blockers to move along the net in order to provide a block.

To complete the play, the hitter must already be approaching the net and be between 3 and 5 feet away from the point of contact when the passed ball reaches the setter's hands (Figure 4.22). It must be remembered that the inside shoot travels a shorter distance and will therefore reach the desired contact point sooner than an outside shoot. In order to compensate, the hitter must begin his or her approach earlier. When executing properly, the hitter attacks crosscourt through the gap between the middle (#3) and the outside (#2) blockers. In many cases neither blocker will have time to react and move to the point of attack. The hitter should therefore have a clean hit against the defensive diggers. Unfortunately, the hitter's angle of approach is very severe, so there is little, if any, possibility of the hitter executing a cut back. This drawback is masked well by the definite possibility of a no-blocker attack, which makes the crosscourt hit very effective.

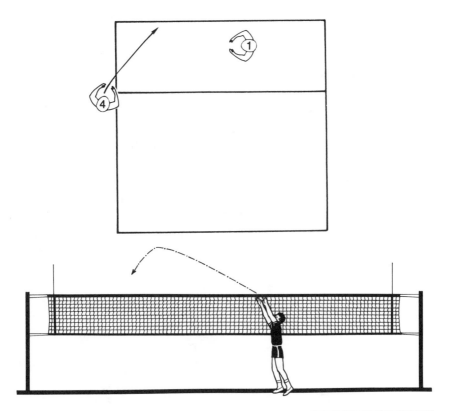

Figure 4.21 The flight of the ball and the path of the attacker's movement for the inside shoot.

Figure 4.22 The hitter should be approximately 3-5 feet away from the point of contact when the ball is in the setter's hands. Using the inside shoot, the hitter should attack between the middle (#3) and outside (#2) blockers.

Back Shoot

This set is executed in a fashion mirroring that of the outside shoot, with the added difficulty of having to backset. The setter must push back a flat and rising set to a point just inside the antenna and approximately 1 foot above the net (Figure 4.23). The outside (#2) hitter in this situation must have begun the approach and be approximately 3-5 feet from point of take off when the ball touches the setter's hands (Figure 4.24).

The hitter should contact the ball just inside the block of the outside defender (#4) and should spike crosscourt. The speed of this set makes it highly unlikely that the middle (#3) blocker would have time to react and assist on the double block. Therefore, the quick set again succeeds in allowing the defense to set up only a single block.

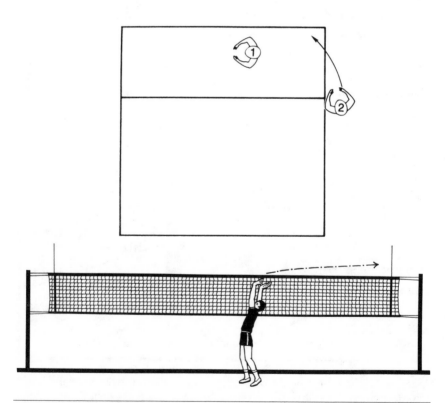

Figure 4.23   The ball is set flat across the net to the approaching (#2) outside hitter.

Figure 4.24 When approaching for the back shoot, the hitter should be approximately 3-5 feet from the point of contact when the ball touches the setter's hands. The hitter should contact the ball just inside the block of the #4 defender.

'A' Quick

This is a set, directed to a point approximately 2 feet above the net, that the middle (#3) hitter will attack (Figure 4.25). As with the high inside set, the ball should be set the same distance from the setter as the setter is from the net. Since this set travels a very short distance, the hitter should be taking his or her last approach step as the ball contacts the setter's hands (Figure 4.26).

The A quick is used to beat the defensive block. The attack is basically right in front of the middle (#3) blocker, so it is necessary to get up and hit the ball before the defender can block it. In this situation again, the hitter faces only a one-player block, as the outside (#2 and #4) blockers have no time to move in and form a two- or three-player block. Even if the middle blocker were to get up in time, the hitter can simply tip or hit the ball around the block.

Back 'A'

This set is almost a mirror image of the A quick (Figure 4.27). The setter backsets a pass to the right outside (#2) hitter in the same

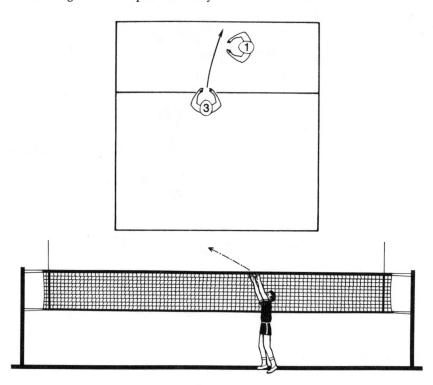

Figure 4.25   The ball is passed as a short rising set to the middle (#3) hitter.

Figure 4.26   The hitter should be taking his or her last step when the ball contacts the setter's hands. Using the A quick, the hitter should beat the middle (#3) blocker to the ball.

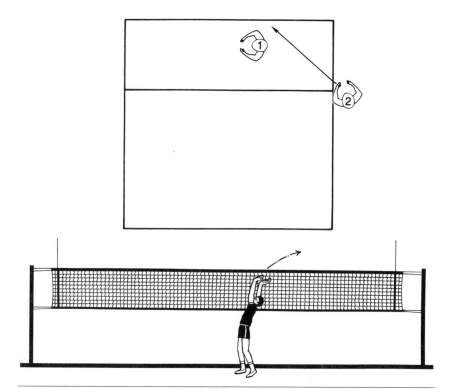

Figure 4.27   The setter backsets a short rising pass to the outside (#2) hitter.

manner as an A quick set is made to the middle (#3) hitter (Figure 4.28). Unlike the A quick, however, the outside hitter does not receive the ball directly in front of any defenders. The point of contact is between the middle (#3) and outside (#2) defensive blockers. The hitter should wait a split second longer to approach and then attack very quickly in order to move before the covering blocker. For an offside hitter, a cut back hit to the right sideline is nearly impossible; consequently, a crosscourt spike should be used between the two blockers. The only defender in a position to stop this attack is the middle (#3) blocker. If the middle blocker anticipates the back A, the middle area would be open and free of blocking. To capitalize on this, the back A could be used to set up the A quick attack and vice versa.

'B' Quick

Here the setter delivers a set to the middle (#3) hitter so that it will be contacted approximately 1 foot above the net (Figure 4.29). The set

Figure 4.28   When approaching for the back A, the hitter should be taking his or her last step when the ball contacts the setter's hands. The ball should be contacted between the middle (#3) and outside (#4) defensive blockers.

must be quicker than that of the A quick because the hitter's approach will begin earlier. The hitter's point of attack along the net again depends upon the position of the setter. However, there is a difference of time in the hitter's approach. For this set to be successful, the hitter should have completed his or her final step, and be beginning to jump, at the moment the passed ball touches the setter's hands (Figure 4.30). In actuality, the ball will be set when the hitter is already airborne.

As with the A quick, this set is used to give the middle (#3) hitter a one-blocker or no-blocker attacking situation. The quickness with which this play is executed makes it impossible for the middle (#3) blocker to get up in time if he or she is watching the set. By the time the ball is set, it will be too late to block. If the blocker instead watches the hitter and is able to set a block, the ball can easily be tipped over or hit around the lone blocker. At the point when the blocker anticipates the B quick set, he or she will be unable to react quickly enough to an outside set. Consequently, you have effectively isolated the middle blocker. The outside blockers cannot react to the middle attack and the middle blocker will be too preoccupied to react to the outside attack. The advantage now is that the threat of a B quick attack from the middle promotes the possibility of all three offensive hitters facing only one-player blocks.

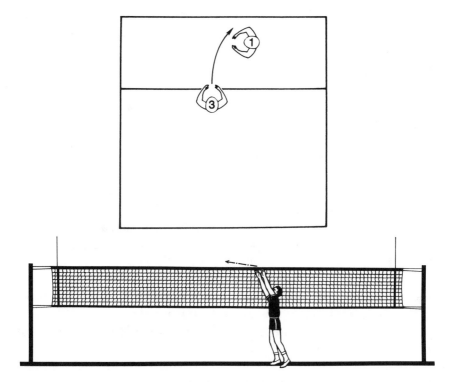

Figure 4.29 The set is a very short and very quick pass to the middle (#3) hitter.

Figure 4.30 The hitter should be beginning his or her jump when the ball touches the setter's hands. Using the B quick the hitter is isolated against the middle blocker in a situation that highly favors the attacker.

It should be becoming clearer now that the success of one setting attack greatly influences the success of other setting attacks. The more setting attacks your team can incorporate into its offense, the more effective that offense will be.

Back 'B'

This set is basically the reverse of the B quick and requires the same if not more coordination between setter and hitter (Figure 4.31). As this is a very quick set and must be executed blindly by the setter, a great deal of practice is required to perfect it. Again, the outside (#2) hitter should have completed the approach and be starting his or her jump when the passed ball touches the setter's hands (Figure 4.32).

The hitter should contact the ball between the middle (#3) and the outside (#4) blockers. As shown in Figure 4.31, the hitter must make his or her final approach on the net at a right angle. If angling in toward the setter instead, there would be little opportunity for the hitter to convert a poor set with his or her upper body twisted and being so near to the setter. However, with the right angled approach on the net, the hitter is able to execute a cut back as well as a crosscourt hit. Hence, the defense must spread itself out in preparation for either of these attacks. Again, the offense has manipulated the defense to its advantage.

Multiple Offense

The multiple offense incorporates all three of the front row hitters in patterns of faking and hitting. The basic theory is that using quick sets alone, the defense will be limited to providing only a one-player block. Using a multiple offense, however, quick sets are combined with fake attacking patterns to enable one of the offensive hitters to face no block at all. In essence, the multiple offense relies upon the faking patterns of nonhitters to draw the defense out of position.

Now that you are using several different sets in many different patterns and combinations, it is necessary to have a simple and effective method of communicating between setter and hitter. To facilitate this, a system of letters and numbers has been established

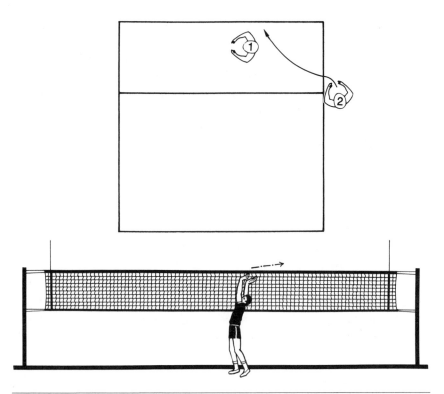

Figure 4.31 The outside (#2) hitter receives a very short and very quick backset from the setter.

Figure 4.32 When the ball touches the setter's hands, the hitter should be starting his or her jump. The ball should be hit between the middle (#3) and the outside (#4) blockers when using the back B set.

with which the chosen play can be described. For each play there is a three-digit code comprised of one letter and two numbers. Each digit of the code has a specific meaning that, when combined with the meanings of the other two digits, provides a detailed instruction for the attacking hitters. The following is an explanation of what the digits mean separately and together in combination.

A)   The first digit of the code is a letter that refers to the position of the player who is to attack the ball.

   L—Left front hitter
   C—Center front hitter
   R—Right front hitter

   The first digit of the code will invariably be one of these three letters (i.e., L, C, or R).

B)   The second digit of the code is a number that refers to a specific area along the length of the net. Figure 4.33 illustrates how the net is broken down into seven distinct areas. Each of these areas is approximately 2 feet in width and the areas are numbered 1 through 7 inclusively.

   Area #1—Area beginning just inside the left antenna.
   Area #2—Area beginning approximately 5 feet inside the left antenna.

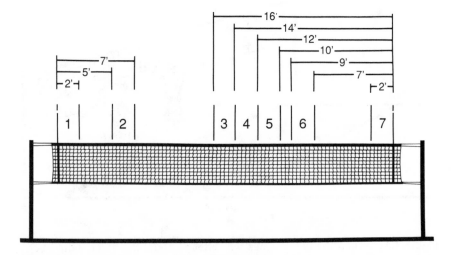

Figure 4.33   Division of the net into 7 distinct areas.

Area #3—Area beginning approximately 4 feet to the left of the setter's position.

Area #4—Area beginning approximately 2 feet to the left of the setter's position.

Area #5—Area beginning immediately to the left of the setter's position.

Area #6—Area beginning immediately to the right of the setter's position.

Area #7—Area beginning just inside the right antenna.

C) The third and final digit of the code refers to the height above the net to which the ball shall be set.

> 1—1 foot above the net
> 2—2 feet above the net
> 3—3 feet above the net
> 4—4 feet above the net
> 5—5 feet above the net
> 6—6 feet or more above the net
> 0—6 feet or more above the net
>> (Note that the final digits 6 and 0 are interchangeable and refer to the same vertical position of the set.)

When you combine the three digits you will have a code that describes (a) the position of the attacking player, (b) the area along the net where the attack will take place, and (c) the height of the set. Therefore, if given the code L-10, you will understand that the left frontcourt hitter will be attacking area #1 on the net and hitting a high (more than 6 feet) set. More simply, the outside (#4) hitter will be hitting a high outside set. The following is a conversion of the various sets previously discussed in this chapter:

High Outside Set	L10 or R70
High Inside Set	C40
Outside Shoot Set	L12
Back Shoot Set	R72
A Quick	C52
Back A	R62
B Quick	C41
Back B	R61

In order to completely supplement this list of sets, there are four more complex setting patterns that involve two or more hitters. These four plays are used extensively in multiple offense and are known as *right cross, fake cross, left inside,* and *left tandem.*

Right Cross

As illustrated in Figure 4.34, the outside (#2) hitter moves laterally behind the setter and crosses over toward the middle of the court (R-43). The middle (#3) hitter begins to approach (C-52) when the outside hitter has reached the area behind the setter's position. The middle hitter now executes the approach for an A quick set. The outside hitter continues to approach, cutting behind and to a position on the net immediately to the left of the middle hitter.

The setter now has two options. The first is an A quick set to the middle hitter, and the second is a set about 1 foot higher and 1 foot farther to the left of the A quick set. If the setter chooses the latter, the middle hitter completes his or her approach and fakes a hit on the ball, thus drawing the block of the middle blocker. It is crucially important that the middle hitter be convincing so that the middle blocker is drawn by the fake. Offensively, the result is that the outside hitter contacts the ball and hits to the left of the preoccupied block. In the right cross, the middle blocker is effectively isolated. The outside (#2) blocker cannot help because he or she must be concerned with the outside (#4) hitter. The outside blocker (#4) cannot help either because he or she is unable to move through the middle blocker who has been faked out of position. The #2 blocker would have to move behind the middle blocker to

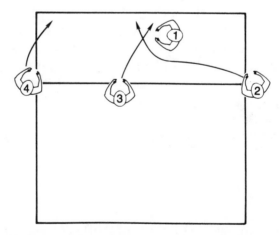

Figure 4.34 The outside (#2) hitter cuts behind and hits to the left of the middle (#3) hitter.

get to the other side, after which time it would be too late to block the offensive hit.

Virtually the only defense against a right cross attack is to switch blocking roles (Figure 4.35), having the blockers switch coverage assignments. Blocker #3 moves laterally to defend the outside (#2) hitter cutting across court, while blocker #4 moves laterally to defend the A quick attack. To be effective, the defense must read this play in advance to allow time for the blockers to switch assignments.

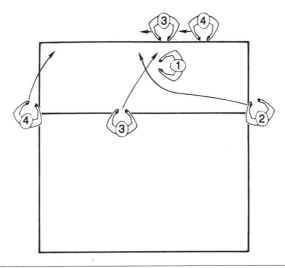

Figure 4.35 Blockers #3 and #4 switch roles in an attempt to stop the right cross.

Fake Cross

If the defense has been exposed to a number of right cross attacks and is adjusting by switching blocking assignments, the offense can attack with a variation of the right cross. As Figure 4.36 depicts, the initial stages of this attack are the same as those for the right cross until the point when the outside (#2) hitter is in the area behind the setter. Once behind the setter, the #2 hitter moves quickly back to the right of the setter for a back A pass (R-62). As a result, the two switching blockers will both be covering the middle (#3) hitter while the outside (#2) hitter faces no block at all. If attempting to stay with the #2 hitter, the #3 blocker has to move around

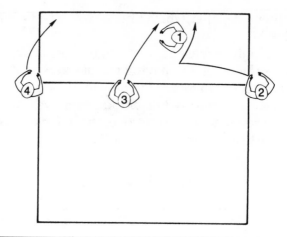

Figure 4.36 The outside (#2) hitter fakes the cross and cuts back to the right for a back A set.

his or her blocking mate (#4). In this instance, the offense has once again manipulated the defense.

Left Inside

This play is used against an anxious or overaggressive middle blocker. The middle (#3) hitter approaches for a B quick set (C-41). Prior to this, the outside (#4) hitter moves forward and cuts sharply

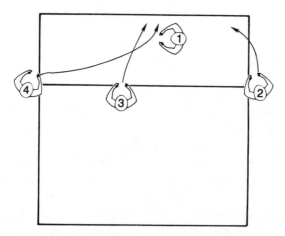

Figure 4.37 The outside (#4) hitter cuts behind and between the #3 hitter and the setter.

toward the middle area, between the setter and the #3 hitter (L-52). The setter sets an A quick to the #4 hitter (Figure 4.37). This play draws the anxious blocker over to defend the #3 hitter, allowing the #4 hitter a clean spike. Again, as in the right cross, this is a situation where the blockers will interfere with each other when attempting to help on the play.

Blocker #4 cannot help as he or she must be concerned with the offside (#2) hitter. Blocker #2 cannot help because blocker #3 is in the way, defending against the fake hitter (#3). Here too, it is necessary for the defense to switch blocking assignments in order to stop this play from succeeding. Likewise, the offense can vary the play by faking and having the #4 hitter attack on the left side of the middle (#3) hitter.

Left Tandem

In this play, the involved offensive players are the outside (#4) hitter and the middle (#3) hitter. As illustrated in Figure 4.38, the #3 hitter approaches as if awaiting a B quick set (C-41). The #4 hitter moves forward a couple of steps and then breaks toward a position directly behind the #3 hitter (L-42). The #4 hitter begins to jump when the #3 hitter is at the peak of his or her jump. In essence, as hitter #4 is going up, hitter #3 will be coming down. If the #3 hitter has faked convincingly, the blocker will also have gone up

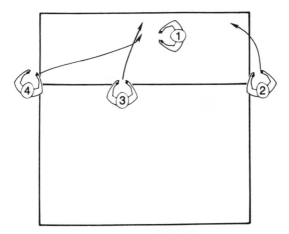

Figure 4.38 The outside (#4) hitter cuts to a position behind that of the middle (#3) hitter.

and come down with him or her. This will allow the setter to pass the ball to the #4 hitter about 1 foot higher and 2 feet farther back than the B quick set. The approaching #4 hitter then hits the ball through the area vacated by the middle blocker.

This attack is indefensible, as help cannot be obtained from either outside blocker due to the fact that the middle blocker has occupied the sole defensive blocking position. It is equally impossible for the middle blocker to jump up in time after having already attempted to block the fake attack. In desperation the middle blocker may choose to wait for the second attacker before attempting to block. In this situation, the setter can simply set the B quick to the first attacker (#3).

Offensive Systems

Perhaps one of the most difficult decisions for a coach to make regards the choice of offensive system to be used. It is crucially important that the system of offense employed by a team be commensurate with the ability of the players of that team. So important is the decision that a criteria-based checklist should be used prior to any final choice. The best system is that which (a) best utilizes the talents of the players involved, (b) best minimizes the exposure of those players' inabilities, (c) is challenging to the players, (d) can be successfully executed by the players, and (e) is compatible with the defensive system to be implemented.

The most prominent difference between offensive systems is the *ratio of hitters to setters*. Therefore, offensive systems are described by this ratio. All offensive systems, save one, are described by two numbers; the first indicates the number of *hitters*, and the second indicates the number of *setters* (e.g., 3-3, 4-2, 5-1). Only one system, the 2-2-2 system, differs. This offensive system employs 2 hitters, 2 universal players, and 2 setters. The following section will detail the similarities and differences among the many types of offensive systems.

The 6-0 System

The 6-0 offensive system uses each player as both a setter and a hitter (Figure 4.39). In this system of play, there are no special-

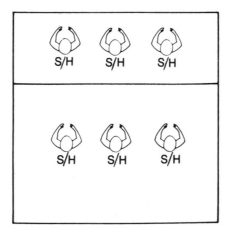

Figure 4.39   Function by position of players in the 6-0 system.

ized positions. Rather, every player is a hitter until rotating to the middle front (#3) position, where each is responsible to set [(Figure 4.40 (i)]. A slightly advanced variation is to designate the right front (#2) position as the setting area [(Figure 4.40 (ii)]. In both instances a two-hitter attack will be used.

It is fundamentally important that young players are not labeled as hitters or setters until they have fully experienced and understand each of these specific positions. Due to its very simplistic nature, the 6-0 system is ideal for beginning players who need exposure to playing in these two basic offensive positions. By affording these players the opportunity to both set and hit, the 6-0

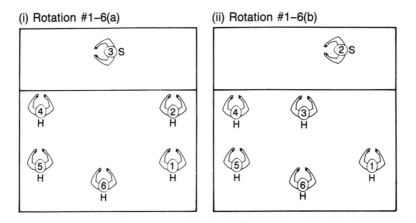

Figure 4.40   (i) The 6-0 system with the setter in position #3. (ii) The 6-0 system with the setter in position #2.

system promotes their development into knowledgeable and fundamentally sound players. Once a player has been initiated through the use of this system, both the player and coach will have a better insight into that player's abilities and affinity for positioning.

The 3-3 System

The 3-3 system represents the simplest system of offense to introduce and incorporate the specialized functions of players. Three players are designated as setters and the remaining three players are designated as hitters. As illustrated in Figure 4.41, the setters and hitters are alternated throughout the rotation (i.e., setter, hitter, setter, hitter, etc.) so that hitters are always separated by a setter and vice versa. In accord with this, the setter always sets from either the middle front (#3) or the right front (#2) positions, depending on his or her position in the rotation. Figures 4.42 (i) through (vi) illustrate the positions of hitters and setters through six rotations. The setter positioned in zone #3 sets from zone #3, and the setter positioned in zone #2 sets from zone #2; hence no switching of positions is required.

The 3-3 system is flexible in that it also allows the setters an opportunity to hit the ball. Whenever there is a setter in zone #2, there is also a setter in zone #4 who is available to hit. This improves both the setting and the hitting skills of the setters without detracting from the development of the hitters. Furthermore, the back-

Figure 4.41 Function and position of players in the 3-3 system.

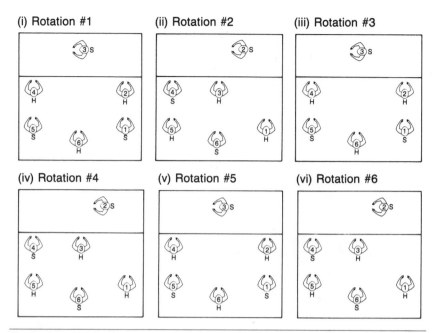

Figure 4.42 (i)-(vi) Positions of setters and hitters through each of the six rotations.

court players develop and improve their passing skills to both the middle and right front setting positions.

The 3-3 system is a very good system for improving the fundamental skills of individual players before exposing them to more advanced systems of play. Although the functions of players are specialized in the 3-3 system, it is not necessary for players to switch or penetrate; this allows players to concentrate completely on the skills at hand. As a result, the 3-3 system can serve as an ideal intermediate step between the simplistic 6-0 system and the more advanced systems that involve switching and penetration.

The 4-2 System

The 4-2 system is perhaps the offensive system most widely used by teams of intermediate to high skill. This system employs four hitters and two setters, with the setters playing opposite each other (Figure 4.43). This ensures that there will always be a setter in the front row while the other is in the back row. It is in the 4-2 system that switching and penetration are added to the specialization of player functions, so it is necessary that the players' level of skill

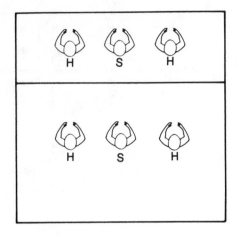

Figure 4.43 Functions and distribution of players in the 4-2 system of offense.

and experience be such that they will be able to cope with the added pressures inherent in this system of play.

It is also in this system that multiple offense attacks can be introduced, because along with the standard two-hitter attack, the

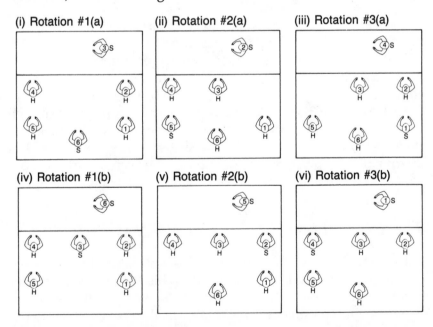

Figure 4.44 (i)-(vi) Position of setters and hitters through each of the first three rotations. There are two options for setter responsibility, (a) and (b), for each of the three rotations.

setter from the back row may penetrate allowing three hitters to attack. This greatly increases the number of offensive attack options. As illustrated in Figure 4.44 (i), (ii), and (iii), the setter may move from the front row to the setting position, providing a two-hitter attack. Conversely, in Figure 4.44 (iv), (v), and (vi), the setter from the back row may penetrate to the setting position, allowing a three-hitter attack. Most often this penetration will occur during serve reception or following a free ball situation that allows the setter the time necessary to penetrate to the net.

The two options of the first rotation are shown in Figure 4.44 (i) and (iv). In rotation #1 (a) [Figure 4.44 (i)], the setter simply moves from the #3 position to zone #2 where he or she will set. In rotation #1 (b) [Figure 4.44 (iv)], the setter penetrates from the #6 position to zone #2 to become the active setter. This allows a three-hitter attack from zones #2(H), #3(S), and #4(H). Rotations #2 and #3 are illustrated in the same manner, showing both a two-hitter attack [#2(a) and #3(a)] and a three-hitter attack [#2(b) and #3(b)]. Rotations #4, 5, and 6 are simply a repeat of rotations #1, 2, and 3 in the same order with the same options.

The 5-1 System

The 5-1 system incorporates only one setter in the lineup with five hitters, at least one of whom should have had some previous setting experience (Figure 4.45). Some teams may have only one capable setter, or they may want to take advantage of one particular setter who is extremely talented. These are the teams most likely to use the 5-1 system. This system makes it necessary for the lone setter to set every offensive play no matter what zone of the court he or she has been rotated to, which requires that the setter be athletically agile and mentally adept. It will be the setter's responsibility to be careful to be in a position to set the offense in every attacking situation. As can be imagined, the setter must also be a very experienced player in order to anticipate all the varied attacking situations. The 5-1 system unfortunately offers few advantages to offset its prominent disadvantages. As a result, few highly skilled teams choose to use the 5-1 system unless it is absolutely necessary.

In the first three rotations, the setter is in the front row [Figure 4.46 (i)-(iii)]. From here the setter moves to zone #2 and sets the

Figure 4.45 Functions and distribution of players in the 5-1 system of offense.

two-hitter attack. It is not until rotations #4, 5, and 6 that a three-hitter attack can be used through the penetration of the setter [Figure 4.46 (iv)-(vi)]. This is a tremendous disadvantage to many high caliber teams who wish to use a multiple offense. For three of the six rotations no such offensive attack is possible.

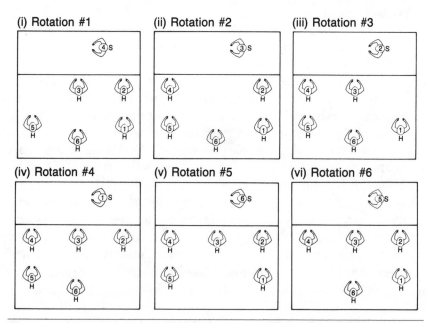

Figure 4.46 (i)-(vi) Position of hitters and setter through each of the first six rotations.

Another detraction of this system is in the pressure it puts on the setter. The setter *must* always be in a position to set. If for some reason the setter were forced to handle the first ball over the net (e.g., dig a spike, receive a serve), he or she would be taken out of the play completely and the offense would be rendered helpless.

Most lower level teams do not have the ability to execute a system that calls for such an exceptionally talented setter. Higher level teams avoid this system as it is very predictable and offers few offensive options, especially when the setter has rotated to the front row. As a result, the 5-1 system is rarely a system of choice and is most often a system of necessity.

The 2-2-2 System

The 2-2-2 system is the most advanced of the offensive systems and accordingly requires players of a high skill level. This system relies on three rather than two types of specialized players. There are two hitters, two setters, and two universal players; the members of each pair are positioned diametrically opposite each other in the rotational order (Figure 4.47). The universal players must be very good all-around athletes who are capable of both hitting and setting with consistency. With this third type of player comes the ability to use a three-hitter attack in every order of the rotation. The 2-2-2 system makes it possible for each of the front row

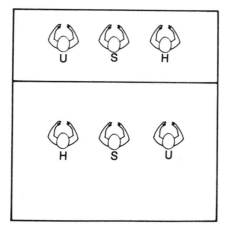

Figure 4.47 Function and distribution of players in the 2-2-2 system of offense.

players to attack, by having either a setter or a universal player from the back row penetrate to the frontcourt setting position. The most desirable area from which a backcourt player can penetrate is zone #1. The second most desirable area is zone #6. The least desirable area from which the setter can penetrate is zone #5 and such penetration should not be attempted unless absolutely necessary.

In each of the first three diagramed rotations [Figure 4.48 (i)-(ix)], there are three options relating to who may set. The rotations designated by an (a) are the simplest, involving the frontcourt setter but allowing only a two-hitter attack. Rotations designated with a (b)

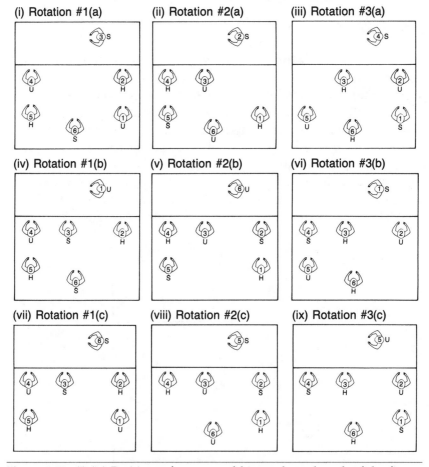

Figure 4.48 (i)-(ix) Positions of setters and hitters through each of the first three rotations. There are three options for setter responsibility, (a), (b), and (c), for each of the three rotations.

are the most desirable for a back row penetration resulting in a three-hitter attack. The least enviable of the back row penetrations allowing a three-hitter attack are those rotations designated by a (c). For instance, rotation #1(a) [Figure 4.48 (i)] illustrates the easiest method of assigning a setter. The front row setter simply moves forward to zone #2. However, this affords only a two-hitter attack and should be used only in cases where a back row player cannot penetrate to set. Rotation #1(b) [Figure 4.48 (iv)] illustrates the easiest method of assigning a backcourt player to penetrate. The universal player penetrates from zone #1 to the frontcourt zone #2 and sets to one of the three available frontcourt hitters. The other option for backcourt penetration is illustrated in rotation #1(c) [Figure 4.48 (vii)].

This option is slightly less desirable than penetration from zone #1 yet is still very acceptable. The setter moves forward to zone #2 from zone #6 and sets to the three frontcourt attackers. The same basic order of options holds for rotations #2 and #3. Rotations #4, 5, and 6 are simply repeats of the first three rotations with all the same options and advantages.

Attack Coverage

As has been discussed, volleyball is a game of transitions and these can occur at almost any point during the game. It follows that once your team has made its third contact, usually a spike, they must be prepared to make the transition to defense. It is important, however, that they do not wait until the opposition has possession of the ball before moving to a defensive position. In some cases this may prove to be too late.

In the event that your hitter should face a good defensive block, the possibility of the ball being deflected back into your court is very high. Therefore it is necessary to prepare defensively while the hitter is in the process of attacking. In actuality, your team must be in both offensive and defensive modes at the same time. This requires a special movement of players to predetermined positions of attack coverage.

Basic Attack Coverage Positions

Once the hitter has initiated his or her approach, five players remain whose task it now is to defend against a blocked ball. Basically, the ball can be blocked in two ways: It can be forced down close to the hitter and the net, or it can be pushed deeper into the back-court area. In order to effectively defend both types of defensive blocks, your players must be arranged so that they can play both short and deep blocks. This requires that the players be set up in a short line attack coverage and a deep line attack coverage.

Short Line Attack Coverage

In order to defend the short block close to the net, you should have a semicircle of two or preferably three players surrounding the at-tacking hitter. The covering players should not crowd too closely in on the hitter, as this would prove more disruptive than helpful. It is desirable that these players start from a deeper position in the court and move slowly forward with the approach of the hitter. This movement allows the covering players the advantage of for-ward momentum if the ball should drop close to the net.

The 6 up defense allows 3 players to form the short line cover-age (Figure 4.49). This is possible because the center back player (#6) is playing very close to the attack line and therefore does not have to move back deep into the court on the transition to defense. However, in the 6 back defense, the center back (#6) player is posi-tioned almost on the baseline and is therefore incapable of providing any close or short coverage on the hitters. As a result, there are few instances when the short line coverage can be made up of 3 players (Figure 4.50).

Deep Line Attack Coverage

The deep line players are positioned in such a way that they fill the deep gaps between the short line coverage. It is not necessary

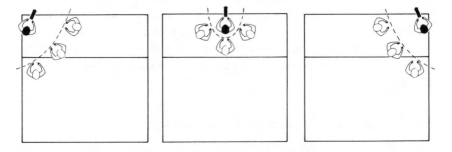

Figure 4.49 6 up, short line coverage for attacks out of the left, middle, and right sides of the court.

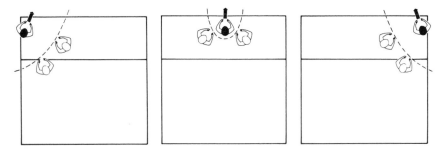

Figure 4.50   6 back, short line coverage for attacks out of the left, middle, and right sides of the court. Note that unlike the coverage with the 6 up, there are only two short line players.

for the deep line coverage to play excessively deep in the court. A defensive block will rarely if ever be so powerful or deep that the players will not have time to move back and play it safely. As most deep blocks reach only the midcourt area at best, this will be the area of concern for the players responsible for deep line coverage.

As the 6 up defense allows three players to form the short line coverage, only two players remain to cover the deep line (Figure 4.51). Conversely, the 6 back defense, due to its two-player short line, enables three players to form the deep line coverage (Figure 4.52).

In the majority of cases, neither the short line nor the deep line players will be able to assume the exact positions illustrated. As often is the case, some of these players may be delayed due to various circumstances. Nevertheless, every attempt should be made by these players to adequately provide coverage for the attacking hitter.

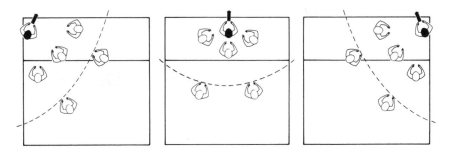

Figure 4.51   6 up, deep line coverage for attacks out of the left, middle, and right sides of the court. The deep line covers the areas between the short line coverage deeper into the midcourt area.

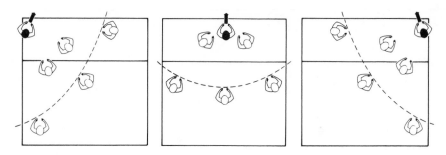

Figure 4.52 6 back deep line coverage for attacks out of the left, middle, and right sides of the court. With only two short line players, the three remaining players are responsible for the deep gaps in the midcourt area.

Importance and Application of Attack Coverage

The importance of attack coverage should never supersede that of defense. Attack coverage plays an important role in the effectiveness and success of a team, but defense is absolutely crucial to that team's effectiveness and success. The emphasis on attack coverage should never be so great that it diminishes the effectiveness of the defense. Therefore, the attack coverage should be designed with the defense in mind. It is important that the coverage be structured so that all individual players can easily make the transitions to and from their defensive positions within the defensive system to be used. For this reason the 6 up and 6 back defensive systems each have different attack coverages.

The following diagrams will illustrate the paths of player movement to be incorporated for each type of defensive system. The illustrations are simple and straightforward, thus little or no explanation is necessary.

Attack Coverage for the 6 Up Defense

The following diagrams illustrate the paths of player movement that may be incorporated in the attack coverage for the 6 up defense.

Two-Hitter Attack With Set From #3 to #4

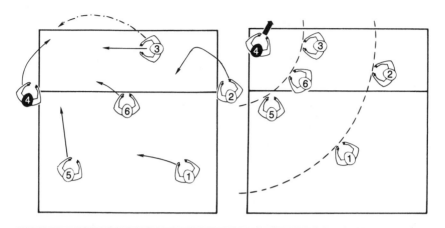

Figure 4.53 Left—Direction of player movement as #3 sets to #4. Right—Final positioning for short and deep line attack coverage.

Two-Hitter Attack With Set From #3 to #2

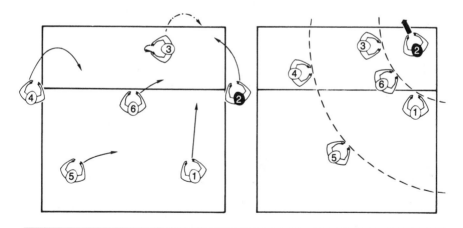

Figure 4.54 Left—Direction of player movement as #3 sets to #2. Right—Final positioning for short and deep line attack coverage.

Two-Hitter Attack With Set From #2 to #4

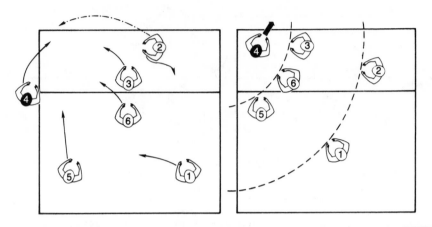

Figure 4.55   Left—Direction of player movement as #2 sets to #4. Right—Final positioning for short and deep line attack coverage.

Two-Hitter Attack With Set From #2 to #3

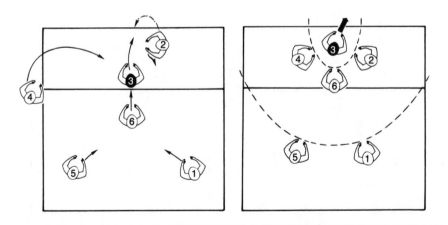

Figure 4.56   Left—Direction of player movement as #2 sets to #3. Right—Final positioning for short and deep line attack coverage.

Three-Hitter Attack With Penetrating Set From #6 to #4

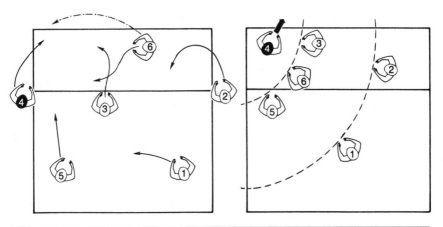

Figure 4.57 Left—Direction of player movement as #6 sets to #4. Right—Final positioning for short and deep line attack coverage.

Three-Hitter Attack With Penetrating Set From #6 to #3

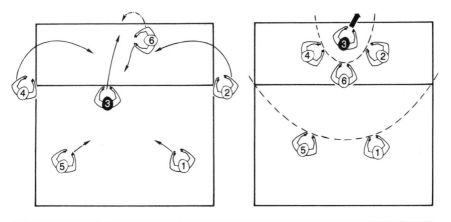

Figure 4.58 Left—Direction of player movement as #6 sets to #3. Right—Final positioning for short and deep line attack coverage.

Three-Hitter Attack With Penetrating Set From #6 to #2

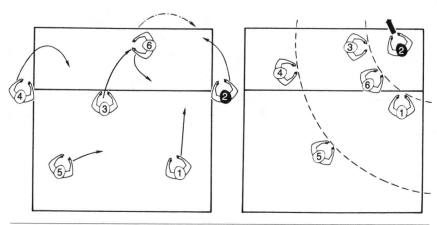

Figure 4.59 Left—Direction of player movement as #6 sets to #2. Right—Final positioning for short and deep line attack coverage.

Attack Coverage for the 6 Back Defense

The following illustrations should clarify the paths of intended player movement when covering the attack within the 6 back defense.

Two-Hitter Attack With Set From #3 to #4

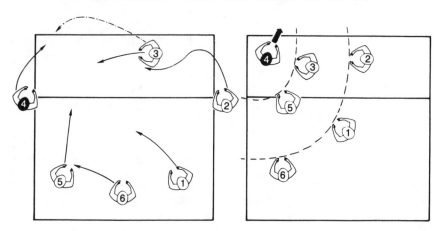

Figure 4.60 Left—Direction of player movement as #3 sets to #4. Right—Final positioning for short and deep line attack coverage.

Two-Hitter Attack With Set From #3 to #2

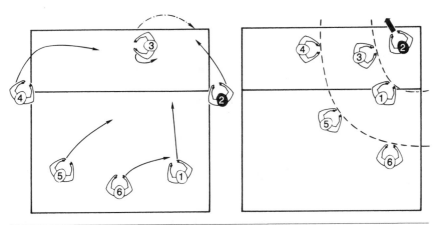

Figure 4.61 Left—Direction of player movement as #3 sets to #2. Right—Final positioning for short and deep line attack coverage.

Two-Hitter Attack With Set From #2 to #4

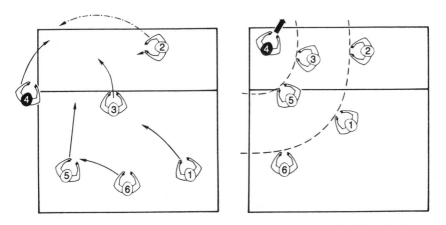

Figure 4.62 Left—Direction of player movement as #2 sets to #4. Right—Final positioning for short and deep line attack coverage.

Two-Hitter Attack With Set From #2 to #3

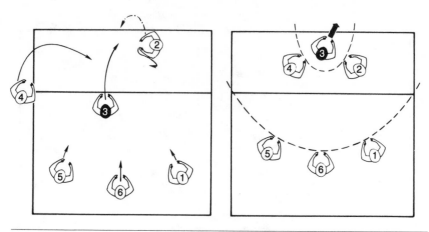

Figure 4.63   Left—Direction of player movement as #2 sets to #3. Right—Final positioning for short and deep line attack coverage.

Three-Hitter Attack With Penetrating Set From #1 to #4

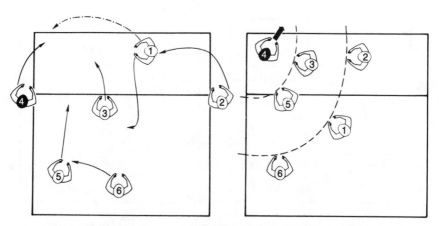

Figure 4.64   Left—Direction of player movement as #1 sets to #4. Right—Final positioning for short and deep line attack coverage.

Three-Hitter Attack With Penetrating Set From #1 to #3

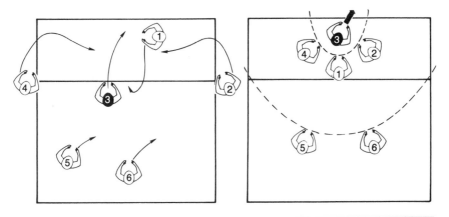

Figure 4.65 Left—Direction of player movement as #1 sets to #3. Right—Final positioning for short and deep line attack coverage. Note that this is one of the few instances in 6 back defense where it is possible to form a three-player short line attack coverage.

Three-Hitter Attack With Penetrating Set From #1 to #2

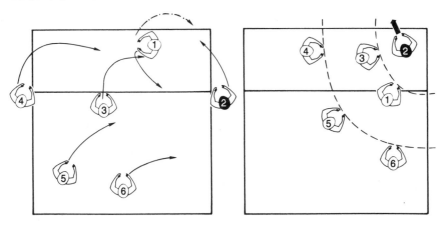

Figure 4.66 Left—Direction of player movement as #1 sets to #2. Right—Final positioning for short and deep line attack coverage.

Chapter 5

Defense

The ultimate priority of defense is to *absorb the opponent's attack so that no point or side out is scored*. Ideally, the defense should handle the opposing attack in such a way that the ball may be set up for a return attack against your opponent. As was evident with the principles of attack coverage, there are two basic lines of defense: the frontcourt line and the backcourt line. The responsibility of the frontcourt players is to block the opposing hitter. The responsibility of the backcourt players is to dig up any ball that may evade the block.

Although the front- and backcourt players function in two completely different ways, they do not function independently of each other. However, it is appropriate to differentiate the independent responsibilities of the front- and backcourt players before discussing their interdependent functions.

Frontcourt Play

Frontcourt play refers to activity in the area between the net and the attack line extending laterally from the left to right sidelines.

The primary players involved in frontcourt play are those positioned in zones #2, #3, and #4. Following are the positional and functional elements specific to the defensive requirements of frontcourt play.

Position of Players

Following the transition period of attack coverage or after an offensive serve, it becomes the primary responsibility of the frontcourt players to block any offensive attack. In order to be adequately prepared to do this, each frontcourt player should be in a position 2-3 feet back from the net (Figure 5.1). Some players may choose to play a little farther off the net so that they can take a step prior to the block jump. This is often the case with poor jumpers or players who have a tendency to commit net violations when playing too close to the net.

Generally, playing too far off the net should be discouraged as it will slow down the defender's ability to put up an effective block. The reaction time consumed when taking the extra step prior to the jump could mean the difference between a defensive block or an offensive kill. Another common problem with playing too far off the net is that the ball can be hit between the blocker and the net, a virtually indefensible play. In the majority of cases, however, deciding where to position the block should be left to the in-

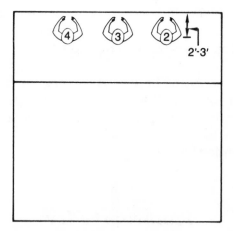

Figure 5.1 Frontcourt blockers should position themselves 2-3 feet back from the net.

dividual player, since the players are the ones who, in the final analysis, can best hide their deficiencies and utilize their abilities.

Deciding where to position along the net is at least equally as important as deciding where to position off the net. The position of blockers along the length of the net almost entirely depends upon what type of blocking system is incorporated. There are basically three types of blocks used to defend the majority of offensive attacks: player to player block, crosscourt block, and line block.

Player to Player Block

Using this type of blocking pattern, each frontcourt player is responsible for blocking the frontcourt opponent opposite him or her. This system generally requires that each blocker be aware of the opponent's most effective hit. The blocker should then defend against that particular attack. If, for instance, the #2 attacker is a very effective crosscourt hitter, the #4 blocker would set up inside the attacker to take that hit away. In this system of blocking, the position of the blockers along the net changes with the movement of the offensive frontcourt hitters. Each of the frontcourt blockers should move laterally along the net in order always to be opposite and slightly inside the attacking opponent (Figure 5.2).

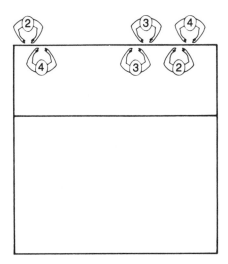

Figure 5.2 Position of players along the net when using the player to player blocking system.

Crosscourt Block

When using this blocking system, the frontcourt players seemingly crowd into the middle area of the court. As illustrated in Figure 5.3, the players position themselves approximately 3 feet apart and between 6 and 8 feet from each sideline.

This system of blocking is used generally against teams whose strength is in the middle of the court or teams who are unable to attack from the full length of the net. The objective of placing the blocking strength in the middle is to stop the crosscourt attacks that invariably pass through the middle court area. There are three inherent advantages of the crosscourt block:

- The crosscourt spike is the most common offensive attack. Therefore, the crosscourt block will be able to stop most attacks.
- If the attack comes from either sideline, the two nearest blockers can move laterally as one unit to the point of attack. As can be imagined, having two players move along the net in the same direction is much more efficient than having them move in opposite directions and meet in the middle. As a result the block will be tighter and ultimately more effective.
- Teams that use a three-hitter attack make nearly all quick sets to the middle, making it advantageous for the strength of your blocking to be there, too.

The crosscourt block is often an effective defense; however, you must be equally prepared to defend outside attacks as well. Upon

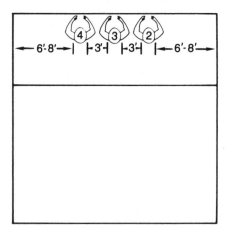

Figure 5.3 Position of frontcourt players along the net for the crosscourt block.

realizing that your team has incorporated the crosscourt block, the opposition will surely increase both the number and frequency of outside attacks.

Line Block

The spacing of the lateral positions of the frontcourt players in this system is the reverse of that for the crosscourt block. In this system, the players are 6-8 feet apart, while the outside players are only about 3 feet from the sidelines (Figure 5.4).

This system of blocking is used primarily to defend against the spike down the sidelines (line spike). It is used against teams with hitters capable of hitting line spikes and teams that effectively use the entire length of the net, generally with a three-hitter attack. The main advantage of the line block is that by being spread out in three basic attacking areas, each of the hitters will be covered by at least one available blocker. This is important against teams who run a lot of quick plays or multiple offenses. It is also possible to execute two-player blocks; however, this requires that the two blockers approach from opposite directions, which makes it difficult for a consistently tight block to be formed.

Types of Blocks

There are basically three different types of blocks, based on the number of defenders involved.

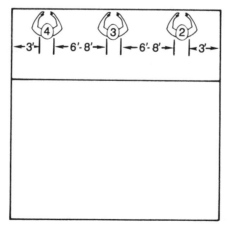

Figure 5.4 Position of frontcourt players along the net for the line block.

One-Player Block

Defensively, the one-player block is perhaps the least desirable, exceeded only by having no block at all. A one-player block is a very narrow deterrent to the attacker as it is extremely easy to hit around. This places an extra burden on the five remaining defensive diggers. The one-player block should generally occur only during quick sets or multiple offense attacks, as when it becomes very difficult to coordinate a two-player block while effectively covering all potential offensive hitters.

Two-Player Block

This block is, in most cases, the most effective block for the defense. The two defenders can create a wall wide enough, in many instances, to stop the attacking hitters. If, however, the hitter should consistently hit around the two-player block, the blockers can "direct" the spike. That is, the defenders create a solid wall in one particular area of the court while leaving another area virtually uncovered. The defensive diggers position themselves in the uncovered area and await the offensive attack. The area behind the blockers is known as the *shadow of the block*. This is the area into which the ball should not be hit directly if the block is solid. Therefore, the hitter is invited to hit to the uncovered area. In anticipation of this, the remaining players can concentrate on a smaller court area into which they can expect the ball to be spiked. It is for these reasons that the two-player block is the most commonly used.

Three-Player Block

This block generally occurs only in the middle attack area. Any effort to move the three-player block to the outside attack areas will be slow and ineffective. This block is used in cases where a very effective hitter is attacking from the middle. The three-player block creates an enormous wall which can only rarely be hit around. However, it does require a great number of players. Once established, this block leaves only three defensive diggers to cover the entire court, a situation that may work to the disadvantage of the defense if a solid block is not formed.

Types of Team Oriented Blocks

These are blocks designed to coordinate the efforts of the frontcourt and the backcourt players. There are basically two types of team oriented blocks.

Player to Player Block

This type of block is very difficult to coordinate between front- and backcourt players, due to the mobile nature of the block. The positioning of the block wholly depends on the positioning of the attacking hitters. As a result, there is a good deal of movement laterally along the net.

The player to player block requires that each frontcourt defender be responsible for the attacker directly opposite him/her. This also includes the responsibility of knowing the hitter's most effective spikes and where and when to position the block to defend against them. The inside hand of the blocker (hand closest to the center of the court) should be directly in front of the hitter's most consistent spike. This will increase the likelihood of a block and ensure that the ball is not wiped off to an area outside the court.

It is because of the flexibility of blocker movement that the player to player block is sometimes used against teams incorporating a multiple offense. By following each hitter, the blockers can position themselves against the quick set attacks (i.e., tandems, crosses, etc.). However, the player to player block is seldom used as the basic type of team block, so the remainder of discussion will be centered around the second type of team block, the area block.

Area Block

The area block is employed in order to force the attackers to hit where the defense wants to receive the ball. The block is set up with the purpose of allowing the attacker to hit around one side of it. That is to say, the blockers strongly block a certain area where they do not want the ball to be hit (e.g., down the sideline), while allowing the attacker to hit freely to an area of the court that is strongly defended (e.g., the crosscourt area). This is the most widely used type of team block, as the defending team can actually manipulate the offense to a degree. By directing the attacker's spike, the defense can advantage itself in many ways:

- By blocking against a certain area, a poor backcourt digger can be hidden from the attackers.
- The crosscourt spike is generally easier to receive than the line spike, and the block can force the crosscourt spike.

- If you have a backcourt setter, the blockers can direct the spike away from that player in order to allow him or her to penetrate.
- Against teams that cannot hit down the line, you can take away the crosscourt spike and force the more difficult line spike.
- You can exaggerate a hitter's weakness by taking away his or her strongest attack with the block.

The following are illustrations and explanations of the various shadows of the area block.

Crosscourt Block Versus Outside Attack.   The crosscourt spike is the easiest and therefore the most common spike in volleyball. It does not require great power or jumping ability to hit this long diagonal spike, a factor that makes it very popular, especially with younger players. As a result, if this spike is taken away, many of these players will be unable to hit a line spike (Figure 5.5). You will in effect nullify their offensive threat.

The crosscourt block must be a tight block with no gap between the two defensive players. In order to preserve the integrity of the block, the left hand of the outside (#2) blocker and the right hand of the middle (#3) blocker should almost be touching. The outside hands of each blocker should be turned inward to prevent a wipe-off hit. The blockers must be positioned just inside the hitter's angle of attack in order to cut off the crosscourt spike. Any ball hit along

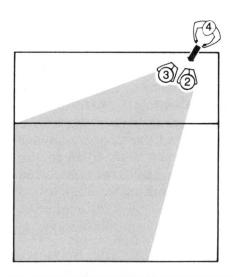

Figure 5.5   Shadow of the crosscourt block against an outside attack.

the sideline or close to the net will be the responsibility of the remaining defensive diggers.

Line Block Versus Outside Attack.   The line spike is one of the most difficult spikes to execute but it is perhaps the most effective. The line spike is directed along the sideline and does not give the defense much of an opportunity to dig it up, as there is usually only one defender in that area. Therefore, if the outside hitter can properly execute this attack, the defense may want to force the more easily defended crosscourt spike. To do so, the defense will set up a line block (Figure 5.6).

The integrity of this block again depends upon the tightness of the two defensive players. Like the crosscourt block, the line block technique requires that the inside hands of the two blockers should almost touch each other. Also, the outside hands, especially that of the outside (#2) blocker, must be turned inward to prevent the wipe-off hit. The only remaining area for the offense to attack is crosscourt, which is considerably easier to defend.

Crosscourt Block Versus Middle Attack.   This block is used against a middle hitter who attacks predominantly with a crosscourt spike. The hitter will usually be right-handed or in some cases left-handed with the ability to cut the ball back. As with all area blocks, the defenders involved must ensure that they close the block by form-

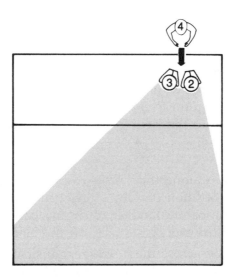

Figure 5.6 Shadow of the line block against an outside attack.

ing up very close together (Figure 5.7). It is therefore the responsibility of the outside (#4) blocker to move along the net and set up beside the middle (#3) blocker. The middle blocker should already be in a position where his or her left hand bisects an imaginary line between the ball and the deep left corner of his or her own court. When both blockers turn their respective outside hands inward, the hitter should have little opportunity to wipe off or hit crosscourt through the block.

Cut Back Block Versus Middle Attack. The shadow created by the cut back block is a mirror image of that created by the crosscourt block (Figure 5.8). This block is implemented to defend teams with a left-handed middle hitter who hits crosscourt or teams with a right-handed hitter who is capable of effectively executing the cut back spike. By having the middle (#3) blocker and the outside (#2) blocker team up in the middle, these attacks can be stopped.

As with the crosscourt block, the cut back block makes it necessary for the middle blocker to set the position for the block. The player does this by ensuring that his or her right hand bisects an imaginary line between the ball and the deep right corner of his or her own court. The outside blocker then moves along the net to a position on the immediate right of the middle blocker. The two blockers now effectively protect the majority of the middle and right side of the defensive court area.

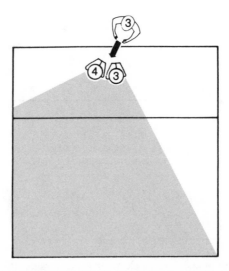

Figure 5.7 Shadow of the crosscourt block against a middle attack.

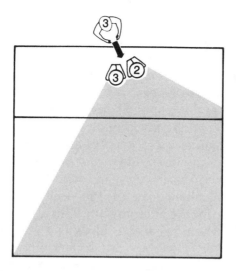

Figure 5.8   Shadow of the cut back block against a middle attack.

Three-Player Block Versus Middle Attack.   This block is designed to defend against a very effective middle hitter. If the two-player block is ineffective or if the middle attacker is very tall or an exceptional hitter, it may be necessary to form a three-player block (Figure 5.9). In essence, the objective of the three-player block is to discourage a full speed spike from the attacker and force him or her

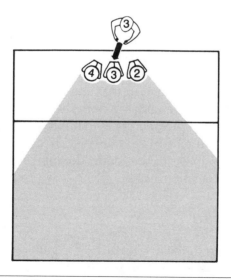

Figure 5.9   Shadow of the three-player block against a middle attack.

to instead hit half-speed or even tip the ball. This is especially necessary if the middle hitter is consistently scoring with spikes that are angled sharply downward over the net. In such a circumstance, the blockers must ensure that additional protection is given to the vulnerable backcourt diggers.

Once again, it is the responsibility of the middle (#3) defender to set the block by taking position directly opposite the attacker's hitting arm. Both outside blockers (#4 and #2) move to the middle area and form up on either side of the middle blocker. The three blockers should jump as one tight and solid unit in order to present as formidable a block as possible. Physically, this block makes it almost impossible for the hitter to score with an unobstructed spike. Psychologically, the three-player block is a great intimidation to the attacking hitter. There are few hitters who would relish the thought of facing a three-player block and fewer still who are capable of consistently scoring against one.

Backcourt Play

Backcourt play refers to activity in the area between the attack line and the baseline extending laterally from the left to right sidelines. It is in zones #5, #6, and #1 that the players primarily involved in backcourt play would be positioned. Following are the positional and functional elements specific to the defensive requirements of backcourt play.

As it is the primary purpose of frontcourt players to block on defense, it follows that the primary purpose of the backcourt players is to play any balls that evade the frontcourt block. In order to best accomplish this, it is important that the position of the backcourt players complement the abilities of both the frontcourt blockers and the backcourt diggers. Relative to the skill of your players, the skill of opponents, and the team's defensive objectives, there are three general formations basic to backcourt defensive positioning. They are 6 up, 6 back, and 6 in line.

6 Up Formation

The 6 up backcourt defensive formation is generally used by teams of lesser skill or experience (Figure 5.10). It is also used against teams who are unable to hit through the block and/or often tip over or

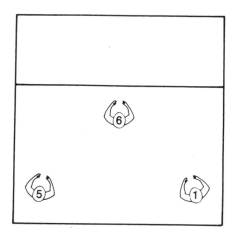

Figure 5.10 Positioning of the backcourt players using the 6 up defensive formation.

around the block. This formation is implemented on the premise that few long powerful hits will be executed by the opposing team and that a great deal of the defense will be against tips or slow looping spikes. Accordingly, the middle (#6) player takes position in the middle of the court approximately 3-4 feet behind the attack line. From this position he or she can quickly and efficiently cover the length of the net against short attacks.

The remaining backcourt area using this formation is the joint responsibility of the outside (#5 and #1) backcourt players. Each will be responsible for the deep crosscourt and line spikes as well as attacks to the deep center area. To accommodate their defensive obligations, the two outside players should position themselves approximately 3-5 feet in from the baseline and about 2-3 feet in from their respective sidelines.

From this basic defensive formation, many slight variations are necessary to adjust to the direction of attack, number of blockers in place, type of team block being used, etc. It is from this fundamental beginning that a more detailed system of defense is formed.

6 Back Formation

This backcourt defensive formation is used by more advanced teams against opponents who are more capable of consistently executing the hard spikes or who seldom attempt to tip over or around the block (Figure 5.11). Anticipating the prowess of the opposing hitters,

Figure 5.11 Positioning of the backcourt players using the 6 back defensive formation.

the middle back (#6) player takes position approximately 2-3 feet in from the baseline. From here, he or she can effectively play the soft blocked balls or the long hard spikes. Unfortunately, as a result of the deep positioning of the middle back player, a very poorly defended area is created immediately behind the block against a middle attack. Herein lies the weakness of the 6 back formation. The only compensation that can be made is to have an experienced and very agile middle back player who is capable of digging both the hard spike and the soft tip.

The remaining two outside (#5 and #1) players position themselves the same distance in from the sidelines (2-3 feet) but slightly closer to the attack line (5-7 feet) than in the 6 up formation. On attacks from the outside, the outside backcourt players are responsible for playing behind the block on their respective sides of the court. In this way, the weakness inherent in defending the middle attack can be avoided by having a player in the area of the block to defend against the slow tip ball.

Despite the apparent weakness of this formation in reference to tip balls behind the block, it is arguably the best court defense against teams with a powerful offensive attack.

6 in Line Formation

This backcourt defensive formation is generally used only by very experienced and highly skilled teams. The positioning of all three backcourt players is approximately 5-7 feet in from the baseline with the outside players approximately 2-3 feet in from their respective sidelines. Using this formation, each backcourt player is primarily responsible for balls spiked into his or her zone (Figure 5.12). The secondary responsibility of the backcourt players is to defend against balls tipped behind the block in their zones. This requires athletes who are capable not only of anticipating the offensive attack but also of executing an effective dive in the event of a short tip over the block. Therefore, because very highly skilled players are needed to execute this defensive formation, this formation should rarely be included in the playbook of teams of only average skill and experience. For this reason, the remaining discussion of defense will involve primarily the 6 up and the 6 back defensive formations.

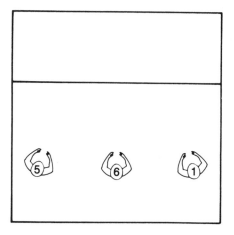

Figure 5.12 Positioning of the backcourt players using the 6 in line defensive formation.

Defensive Team Play— 6 Up and 6 Back Systems

At this point, you should be aware of the independent functions and responsibilities of the front- and backcourt players. Indeed the front- and backcourt players operate as two distinct units with their respective independent functions. However, in the context of a team game, the independent functions of one player are interdependent with the independent functions of the remaining players. So both the front- and backcourt players must be prepared to function as one complete defensive team unit rather than as two separate bodies of individuals, and all six defensive players must function inter- dependently while carrying out their independent responsibilities. The following section demonstrates the movement of players in both the 6 up and 6 back defensive systems while facing attacks from a number of different areas.

6 Up Defense
Defending the Outside Attack With a Crosscourt Block

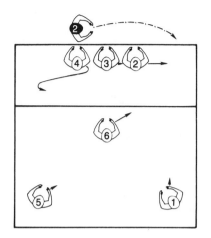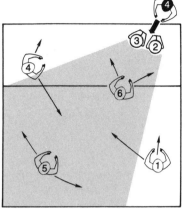

Figure 5.13 Left—Direction of player movement in preparation for defending against an outside attack. Right—Final positioning and areas of responsibility when blocking crosscourt and using a 6 up defense.

Player—Movement	Player—Responsibilities
#1—moves up the sideline toward the area of the block.	#1—responsible for spikes down the right sideline or balls tipped into the area behind #6.
#4—moves off the net to an area close to the attack line.	#4—responsible for any deep tips behind #6 and for sharply cut spikes inside the attack line.
#5—moves laterally toward the area of attack.	#5—responsible for all long crosscourt spikes in the areas of both the left sideline and the baseline.
#6—moves over with the set to an area on the attack line behind the block.	#6—responsible for any short tip balls behind the block or for any ball that is wiped off the block.

6 Up Defense
Defending the Outside Attack With a Line Block

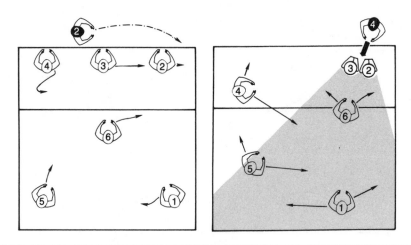

Figure 5.14 Left—Direction of player movement in preparation for defending against an outside attack. Right—Final positioning and areas of responsibility when blocking line and using a 6 up defense.

Player—Movement	Player—Responsibilities
#1—moves laterally across the baseline to an area slightly right of the middle.	#1—responsible for any balls directed into the deep baseline area.
#4—moves off the net with the set to an area close to the attack line.	#4—responsible for any deep tips behind #6 and for sharply cut spikes inside the attack line.
#5—moves up the sideline with the set forming a diagonal line between him- or herself, the ball and the #3 blocker.	#5—responsible for spikes inside the block and balls hit behind #4 and in front of #1.
#6—moves over with the set to an area on the attack line behind the block.	#6—responsible for any short tip balls behind the block or any ball that is wiped off the block.

6 Up Defense
Defending the Middle Attack With a Crosscourt Block

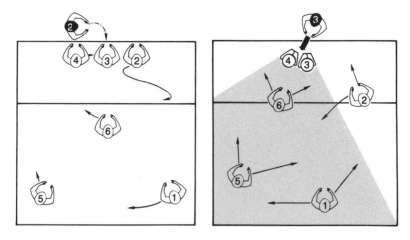

Figure 5.15 Left—Direction of player movement in preparation for defending against a middle attack. Right—Final positioning and areas of responsibility when blocking crosscourt and using a 6 up defense.

Player—Movement

#1—moves laterally across the baseline to an area just to the right of the middle.

#2—moves off the net with the set to an area on the attack line to the right of the block.

#5—moves forward along the sideline to an area in line with the ball and the block.

#6—moves forward and to the left to an area on the attack line directly behind the block.

Player—Responsibilities

#1—responsible for spikes deep into the backcourt baseline area.

#2—responsible for spikes inside the attack line and tips in the area to the right of the block.

#5—responsible for any balls hit inside the block and balls hit behind #6 and in front of #1.

#6—responsible for any short tip balls behind the block or any ball that is wiped off the block.

6 Up Defense
Defending the Middle Attack With a Cut Back Block

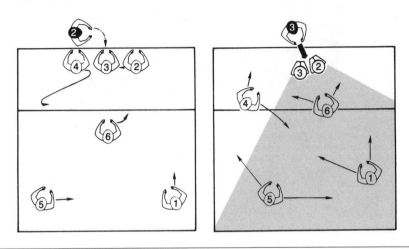

Figure 5.16 Left—Direction of player movement in preparation for defending against a middle attack. Right—Final positioning and areas of responsibility when using a cut back block and a 6 up defense.

Player—Movement	**Player—Responsibilities**
#1—moves forward along the sideline to an area in line with the ball and the #2 blocker.	#1—responsible for spikes inside the block and balls hit behind #6 and in front of #5.
#4—moves off the net with the set to an area on the attack line to the left of the block.	#4—responsible for spikes inside the attack line and tips in the area to the left of the block or just behind #6.
#5—moves laterally along the baseline to an area slightly left of the middle.	#5—responsible for spikes deep into the backcourt baseline area.
#6—moves forward and to the right to an area on the attack line directly behind the block.	#6—responsible for any short tip balls behind the block or any ball that is wiped off the block.

6 Up Defense
Defending the Middle Attack With a Three-Player Block

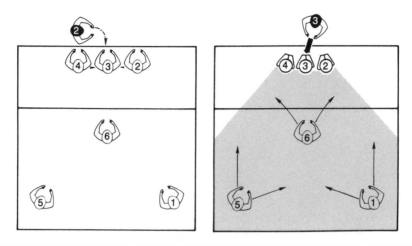

Figure 5.17 Left—Direction of player movement in preparation for defending against a middle attack. Right—Final positioning and areas of responsibility when using a three-player block and a 6 up defense.

Player—Movement	Player—Responsibilities
#1—holds position in the 6 up formation.	#1—responsible for spikes into the deep right corner or balls hit over the head of #6.
#5—holds position in the 6 up formation.	#5—responsible for spikes into the deep left corner or balls hit over the head of #6.
#6—holds position in the 6 up formation.	#6—responsible for the entire area around the block into which a ball may be tipped or wiped off the block.

6 Back Defense
Defending the Outside Attack With a Crosscourt Block

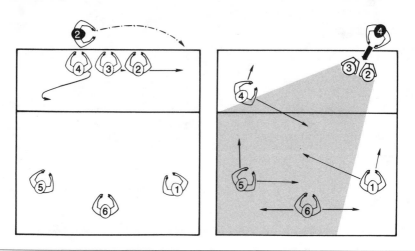

Figure 5.18 Left—Direction of player movement in preparation for defending against an outside attack. Right—Final positioning and areas of responsibility when blocking crosscourt and using a 6 back defense.

Player—Movement	Player—Responsibilities
#1—holds position of the 6 back formation.	#1—responsible for spikes down the line and balls hit into the midcourt area behind #4's and in front of #5's area of responsibility.
#4—moves off the net with the set to an area close to the attack line and to the left of the block.	#4—responsible for spikes inside the attack line and balls tipped in the area behind the block.
#5—holds position of the 6 back formation with some movement to line up with the block.	#5—responsible for crosscourt spikes over the block and the areas behind #4 and in front of #6.
#6—holds position of the 6 back formation.	#6—responsible for all balls hit in the deep baseline area.

6 Back Defense

Defending the Outside Attack With a Line Block

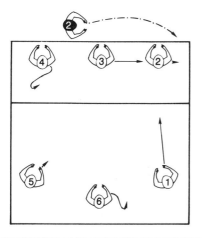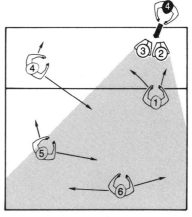

Figure 5.19 Left—Direction of player movement in preparation for defending against an outside attack. Right—Final positioning and areas of responsibility when blocking line and using a 6 back defense.

Player—Movement	Player—Responsibilities
#1—moves forward along the sideline to a position just behind the attack line and the block.	#1—responsible for any short tip balls behind the block or for any ball that is wiped off the block.
#4—moves off the net with the set to an area close to the attack line and to the left of the block.	#4—responsible for spikes inside the attack line and balls hit into the midcourt area behind the attack line.
#5—moves ahead and to the right to a position in line with the ball and the #3 blocker.	#5—responsible for long spikes inside the block and the area in front of #6 and behind #4.
#6—moves laterally across the baseline to an area just right of the middle.	#6—responsible for all balls hit to the deep baseline area and the deep right sideline area.

6 Back Defense
Defending the Middle Attack With a Crosscourt Block

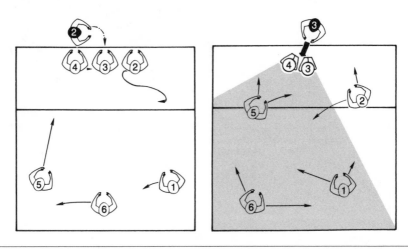

Figure 5.20 Left—Direction of player movement in preparation for defending against a middle attack. Right—Final positioning and areas of responsibility when blocking crosscourt and using a 6 back defense.

Player—Movement	**Player—Responsibilities**
#1—moves laterally to the left to an area just right of the middle.	#1—responsible for spikes to the right sideline and deep right corner, and the area in front of #6.
#2—moves off the net with the set to a position near the attack line to the right of the block.	#2—responsible for any tips behind #5 and for sharply cut spikes inside the attack line to the right of the block.
#5—moves forward along the sideline to a position on the attack line behind and to the left of the block.	#5—responsible for any short tip balls behind the block or any ball that is wiped off the block.
#6—moves laterally across the baseline almost to the left sideline to a position in line with the ball and the block.	#6—responsible for any deep spike over the block to the left sideline and baseline areas.

6 Back Defense
Defending the Middle Attack With a Cut Back Block

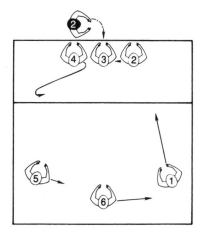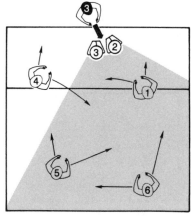

Figure 5.21 Left—Direction of player movement in preparation for defending against a middle attack. Right—Final positioning and areas of responsibility when using a cut back block and a 6 back defense.

Player—Movement	**Player—Responsibilities**
#1—moves forward along the sideline to a position on the attack line behind and to the right of the block.	#1—responsible for any short tip balls behind the block or any ball that is wiped off the block.
#4—moves off the net with the set to a position near the attack line to the left of the block.	#4—responsible for any tips behind #1 and for sharply cut spikes inside the attack line to the left of the block.
#5—moves laterally to the right to an area just left of the middle.	#5—responsible for spikes to the left sideline and deep left corner and the area in front of #6.
#6—moves laterally across the baseline almost to the right sideline to a position in line with the ball and the block.	#6—responsible for any deep spike over the block to the left sideline and baseline areas.

6 Back Defense
Defending the Middle Attack With a Three-Player Block

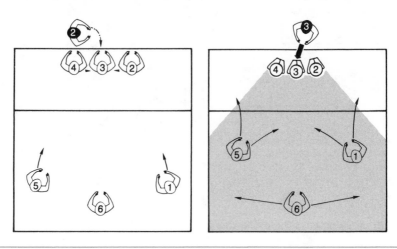

Figure 5.22 Left—Direction of player movement in preparation for defending against a middle attack. Right—Final positioning and areas of responsibility when using a three-player block and a 6 back defense.

Player—Movement	**Player—Responsibilities**
#1—moves forward along the sideline to a position at center court.	#1—responsible for balls hit in the center area or tip balls short and to the right of the block.
#5—moves forward along the sideline to a position at center court.	#5—responsible for balls hit in the center area or tip balls short and to the left of the block.
#6—holds position of the 6 back formation.	#6—responsible for the entire backcourt and baseline areas.

Variations of the 6 Back
Defensive System

The 6 up and 6 back defenses are the two basic defensive systems. However, there are circumstances when specialized variations of these defenses prove more effective. There are three variations that will be described, each of which is designed with very specific objectives in mind. The following section will discuss and illustrate these three variations: the frontcourt slide defense, the backcourt slide defense, and the pinch defense.

Frontcourt Slide Defense

This defensive system requires that the nonblocking frontcourt player slide laterally across the court to a position behind the block. This leaves three defensive diggers in the deep court area while the nonblocking frontcourt player is free to cover any tip balls around the block.

The frontcourt slide defense is generally used by teams with a tall, solid block or teams who are facing opponents who have a tendency to tip over the block as a result of their inability to hit through it. A disadvantage of this system is that the nonblocking frontcourt player, who must slide over behind the block, will be out of position should the transition from defense to offense be made. Consequently, the player executing the frontcourt slide must be very agile and able to return quickly to the offensive attacking position. Figures 5.23 through 5.27 illustrate the application of the frontcourt slide defense against both outside and middle attacks using various blocking formations.

Frontcourt Slide Defense
Defending the Outside Attack With a Crosscourt Block

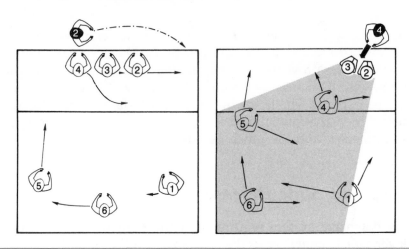

Figure 5.23 Left—Direction of player movement in preparation for defending against an outside attack. Right—Final positioning and areas of responsibility when blocking crosscourt and using a frontcourt slide defense.

Player—Movement	Player—Responsibilities
#1—moves laterally to a position directly in line with the block.	#1—responsible for spikes to the right sideline area, the right baseline area, and the area in front of #6.
#4—moves off the net with the set to a position on the attack line behind the block.	#4—responsible for any short tip balls behind the block or any ball that is wiped off the block.
#5—moves forward along the sideline to a position just behind the attack line.	#5—responsible for spikes inside the attack line and balls hit in the area behind #4.
#6—moves laterally across the baseline to a position in line with the ball and the block.	#6—responsible for spikes deep into the left corner and balls hit into the right sideline and baseline areas.

Frontcourt Slide Defense
Defending the Outside Attack With a Line Block

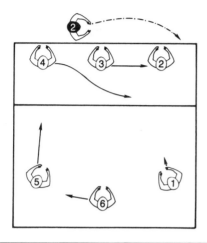 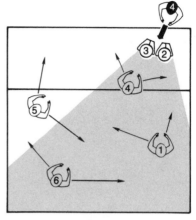

Figure 5.24 Left—Direction of player movement in preparation for defending against an outside attack. Right—Final positioning and areas of responsibility when blocking line and using a frontcourt slide defense.

Player—Movement	Player—Responsibilities
#1—moves forward along the sideline to an area approximately at center court.	#1—responsible for balls hit into the shallow right sideline area and balls hit behind #4 and in front of #5.
#4—moves off the net with the set to a position on the attack line behind the block.	#4—responsible for any short tip balls behind the block or any ball that is wiped off the block.
#5—moves forward along the sideline to a position slightly behind the attack line.	#5—responsible for spikes inside the attack line and balls hit in the area behind #1 and in front of #6.
#6—moves laterally across the baseline to a position in line with the ball and the block.	#6—responsible for deep spikes over the block, balls hit to the deep left sideline, and the entire baseline area.

Frontcourt Slide Defense
Defending the Middle Attack With a Crosscourt Block

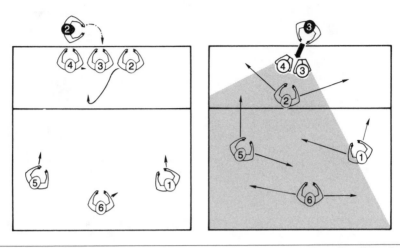

Figure 5.25 Left—Direction of player movement in preparation for defending against a middle attack. Right—Final positioning and areas of responsibility when blocking crosscourt and using a frontcourt slide defense.

Player—Movement	**Player—Responsibilities**
#1—moves forward along the sideline to a position at center court.	#1—responsible for spikes to the right sideline area and balls hit in the area behind #2 and in front of #5.
#2—moves off the net with the set to a position on the attack line directly behind the block.	#2—responsible for any short tip balls behind the block or any ball that is wiped off the block.
#5—moves forward along the sideline to a position at center court.	#5—responsible for spikes to the left sideline area as well as balls hit into the area in front of #6 and behind #1. Also responsible for the area to the left of #2.
#6—moves slightly forward and to the right to a position directly in line with the #3 blocker.	#6—responsible for any deep spikes to the entire baseline area including both deep sideline corners.

Frontcourt Slide Defense
Defending the Middle Attack With a Cut Back Block

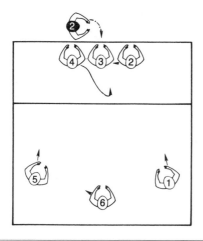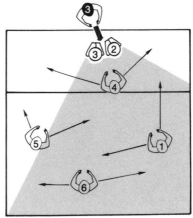

Figure 5.26 Left—Direction of player movement in preparation for defending against a middle attack. Right—Final positioning and areas of responsibility when using a cut back block and a frontcourt slide defense.

Player—Movement	**Player—Responsibilities**
#1—moves forward along the sideline to a position at center court.	#1—responsible for spikes to the right sideline area as well as balls hit into the area in front of #6 and behind #5. Also responsible for the area to the right of #4.
#4—moves off the net with the set to a position on the attack line directly behind the block.	#4—responsible for any short tip balls behind the block or any ball that is wiped off the block.
#5—moves forward along the sideline to a position at center court.	#5—responsible for spikes to the left sideline area and balls hit in the area behind #4 and in front of #1.
#6—moves slightly forward and to the left to a position directly in line with the #3 blocker.	#6—responsible for any deep spikes to the entire baseline area including both deep sideline corners.

Frontcourt Slide Defense
Defending the Middle Attack With a Three-Player Block

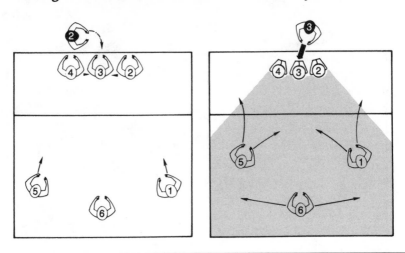

Figure 5.27 Left—Direction of player movement in preparation for defending against a middle attack. Right—Final positioning and areas of responsibility when using a three-player block and a frontcourt slide defense.

Player—Movement	Player—Responsibilities
#1—moves forward along the sideline to a position at center court.	#1—responsible for balls hit in the center area or tip balls short and to the right of the block.
#5—moves forward along the sideline to a position at center court.	#5—responsible for balls hit in the center area or tip balls short and to the left of the block.
#6—holds position of the 6 back formation.	#6—responsible for the entire backcourt and baseline areas.

Backcourt Slide Defense

This system of defense requires that the backcourt player who is in line with the block move forward to a position behind the block. As with the frontcourt slide defense, the player who has moved in behind the block will be ready to play any balls tipped in the area of the block.

Also like the frontcourt slide defense, this system is used by teams with a tall, solid block, or by teams that face opponents who tend to tip over the block as a result of their inability to hit through it. However, unlike the frontcourt slide defense, the nonblocking frontcourt player is not taken out of position. Rather, this player remains in the vicinity of his or her attacking area in preparation for the transition to offense. Figures 5.28 through 5.32 illustrate the application of the backcourt slide defense against both outside and middle attacks using various blocking formations.

Backcourt Slide Defense
Defending the Outside Attack With a Crosscourt Block

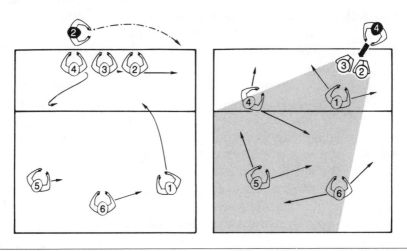

Figure 5.28 Left—Direction of player movement in preparation for defending against an outside attack. Right—Final positioning and areas of responsibility when blocking crosscourt and using a backcourt slide defense.

Player—Movement	**Player—Responsibilities**
#1—moves forward along the sideline to a position on the attack line directly behind the block.	#1—responsible for any short tip balls behind the block or any ball that is wiped off the block.
#4—moves off the net with the set to a position close to the attack line off the inside shoulder of blocker #3.	#4—responsible for spikes inside the attack line and balls tipped in the area behind #1 and in front of #5.
#5—moves laterally to a position in line with the ball and the block.	#5—responsible for crosscourt spikes over the block, balls hit in front of #6, and balls hit into the areas behind #4.
#6—moves forward and to the right to a position directly in line and behind blocker #3.	#6—responsible for the deep right sideline area as well as the entire baseline area.

Backcourt Slide Defense
Defending the Outside Attack With a Line Block

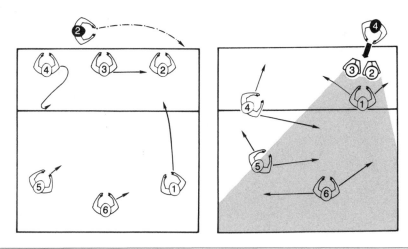

Figure 5.29 Left—Direction of player movement in preparation for defending against an outside attack. Right—Final positioning and areas of responsibility when blocking line and using a backcourt slide defense.

Player—Movement	Player—Responsibilities
#1—moves forward along the sideline to a position on the attack line directly behind the block.	#1—responsible for any short tip balls behind the block or any ball that is wiped off the block.
#4—moves off the net with the set to a position on the attack line off the left shoulder of the #3 blocker.	#4—responsible for spikes inside the attack line and balls tipped into the area behind #1 and in front of #5.
#5—moves forward and to the right to a position in line with the ball and the #3 blocker.	#5—responsible for crosscourt spikes over the block, balls hit in front of #6, and balls hit into the areas behind #4.
#6—moves ahead and to the right to a position just right of the middle.	#6—responsible for the deep right sideline area as well as the entire baseline area.

Backcourt Slide Defense
Defending the Middle Attack With a Crosscourt Block

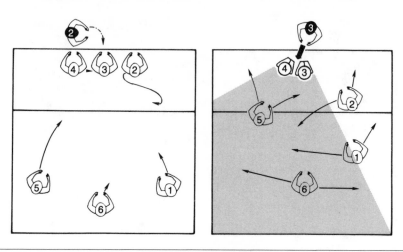

Figure 5.30 Left—Direction of player movement in preparation for defending against a middle attack. Right—Final positioning and areas of responsibility when blocking crosscourt and using a backcourt slide defense.

Player—Movement	**Player—Responsibilities**
#1—moves forward along the sideline to a position at center court.	#1—responsible for any balls hit behind #2 and balls directed toward the area in front of #6.
#2—moves off the net with the set to a position just inside the attack line to the right of the block.	#2—responsible for any balls hit into the area right of the block as well as the area in front of #1 and behind #5.
#5—moves forward along the sideline to a position on the attack line behind the block.	#5—responsible for any short tip balls behind the block or any ball that is wiped off the block.
#6—moves forward and to the right to a position directly in line with and behind #3.	#6—responsible for all deep balls directed anywhere in the back third of the court.

Backcourt Slide Defense
Defending the Middle Attack With a Cut Back Block

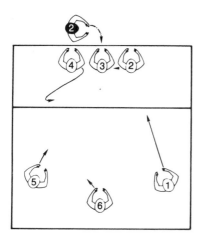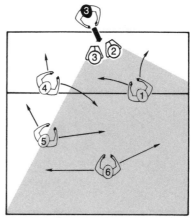

Figure 5.31 Left—Direction of player movement in preparation for defending against a middle attack. Right—Final positioning and areas of responsibility when using a cut back block and a backcourt slide defense.

Player—Movement	**Player—Responsibilities**
#1—moves forward along the sideline to a position on the attack line behind the block.	#1—responsible for any short tip balls behind the block or any ball that is wiped off the block.
#4—moves off the net with the set to a position just inside the attack line to the left of the block.	#4—responsible for any balls hit into the area left of the block as well as the area in front of #5 and behind #4.
#5—moves forward along the sideline to a position at center court.	#5—responsible for any balls hit behind #4 and balls directed toward the area in front of #6.
#6—moves forward and to the left to a position directly in line with and behind blocker #3.	#6—responsible for all deep balls directed anywhere in the back third of the court.

Backcourt Slide Defense
Defending the Middle Attack With a Three-Player Block

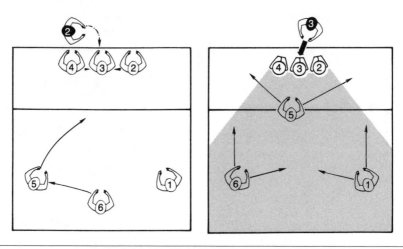

Figure 5.32 Left—Direction of player movement in preparation for defending against a middle attack. Right—Final positioning and areas of responsibility when using a three-player block and a backcourt slide defense.

Player—Movement	**Player—Responsibilities**
#1—holds position of the 6 back formation.	#1—responsible for spikes into the right sideline and center areas.
#5—moves forward and to the right to a position on the attack line behind the block.	#5—responsible for the entire area around the block into which the ball may be tipped or wiped off the block.
#6—moves laterally left to take over the position vacated by #5.	#6—responsible for spikes into the left sideline and center areas.

Pinch Defense

This defensive system is used by teams who wish to protect their middle court area. If the opponent attacks crosscourt or has a tendency to play a great deal of tip balls over or around the block, this system will be very effective.

The pinch defense basically requires that all nonblocking players move in or "pinch" behind the block. In effect, the pinch defense simply resembles a shallow 6 back system. This system is also effective if the blockers are unable to consistently form a tight block. This middle oriented defense will be in a position to dig attacks through the middle area. Figures 5.33 through 5.37 illustrate the application of the pinch defense against both outside and middle attacks using various blocking formations.

Pinch Defense
Defending the Outside Attack With a Crosscourt Block

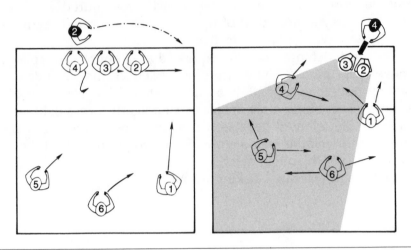

Figure 5.33 Left—Direction of player movement in preparation for defending against an outside attack. Right—Final positioning and areas of responsibility when blocking crosscourt and using a pinch defense.

Player—Movement	Player—Responsibilities
#1—moves forward along the sideline to a position just behind the attack line off the right shoulder of blocker #2.	#1—responsible for any short tip balls in the area behind and right of the block.
#4—moves off the net with the set to the middle left area just short of the attack line.	#4—responsible for any short tip balls in the area behind and left of the block and behind #1.
#5—moves forward and to the right to a position in line with the ball and the block.	#5—responsible for crosscourt spikes over the block, balls hit in front of #6, and balls hit into the areas behind #4.
#6—moves forward and to the right to a position directly in line with and behind blocker #3.	#6—responsible for balls hit to the right sideline and entire deep third of the backcourt.

Pinch Defense
Defending the Outside Attack With a Line Block

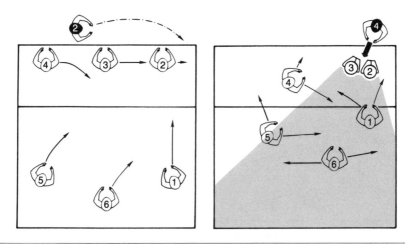

Figure 5.34 Left—Direction of player movement in preparation for defending against an outside attack. Right—Final positioning and areas of responsibility when blocking line and using a pinch defense.

Player—Movement	Player—Responsibilities
#1—moves forward along the sideline to a position just behind the attack line and directly behind blocker #2.	#1—responsible for any short tip balls behind the block or any ball that is wiped off the block.
#4—moves off the net with the set to a position in the middle left area just short of the attack line.	#4—responsible for any short tip balls in the area to the left of the block and behind #1.
#5—moves forward and to the right to a position in line with the ball and the block.	#5—responsible for crosscourt attacks, balls hit in front of #6, and balls hit into the areas behind #4.
#6—moves forward and to the right to a position in line with the left shoulder of blocker #3.	#6—responsible for balls hit to the right sideline area and the entire deep third of the backcourt.

Pinch Defense
Defending the Middle Attack With a Crosscourt Block

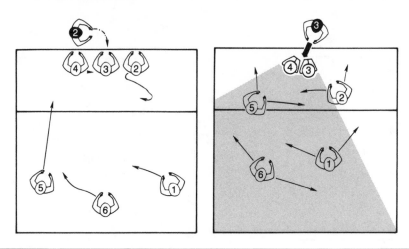

Figure 5.35 Left—Direction of player movement in preparation for defending against a middle attack. Right—Final positioning and areas of responsibility when blocking crosscourt and using a pinch defense.

Player—Movement	**Player—Responsibilities**
#1—moves forward and to the left to a position near midcourt in line with the right shoulder of blocker #3.	#1—responsible for balls hit into the area behind #5 and the entire right sideline.
#2—moves off the net with the set to a position just inside the attack line to the right of the block.	#2—responsible for any short tip balls directed to the areas behind or to the right of the block.
#5—moves forward along the sideline to a position just inside the attack line to the left of the block.	#5—responsible for balls hit behind #2 or the area to the left of the block.
#6—moves forward and to the left to a position in line with the ball and the block.	#6—responsible for attacks crosscourt, the left sideline and the baseline area behind #1.

Pinch Defense
Defending the Middle Attack With a Cut Back Block

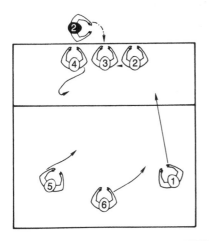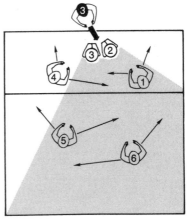

Figure 5.36 Left—Direction of player movement in preparation for defending against a middle attack. Right—Final positioning and areas of responsibility when using a cut back block and a pinch defense.

Player—Movement	Player—Responsibilities
#1—moves forward along the sideline to a position just inside the attack line to the right of the block.	#1—responsible for any short tip balls directed to the areas behind or to the right of the block.
#4—moves off the net with the set to a position just inside the attack line and to the left of the block.	#4—responsible for balls hit behind #1 or the area to the left of the block.
#5—moves forward and to the right to a position near midcourt and in line with the left shoulder of the #3 blocker.	#5—responsible for attacks directed in front of #6 or the areas behind #4.
#6—moves forward and to the right to a position in line with the ball and the block.	#6—responsible for attacks crosscourt, the right sideline, and the baseline area behind #5.

Pinch Defense
Defending the Middle Attack With a Three-Player Block

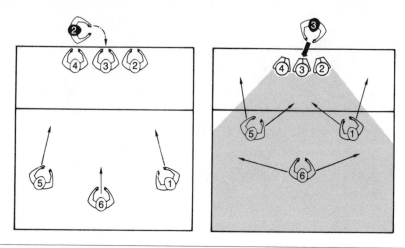

Figure 5.37 Left—Direction of player movement in preparation for defending against a middle attack. Right—Final positioning and areas of responsibility when using a three-player block and a pinch defense.

Player—Movement	Player—Responsibilities
#1—moves forward along the sideline to a position just behind the attack line and to the right of the block.	#1—responsible for the areas behind and to the right of the block.
#5—moves forward along the sideline to a position just behind the attack line and to the left of the block.	#5—responsible for the areas behind and to the left of the block.
#6—moves forward to a position in the center of the backcourt.	#6—responsible for the areas behind #1 and #5 as well as the entire deep third of the backcourt.

Free Ball Defense

There are occasions when the opposition is unable to execute an offensive spike attack. The result of this is either a "free" ball or a "down" ball. A free ball situation occurs if a poor set is made that the attacker is unable to spike, or if the ball has been misplayed, forcing the opposition to weakly pass the ball over the net. As a result of either offensive misfortune, the defense expects an easy pass referred to as a free ball.

A down ball situation occurs when a set is too far off the net but the attacker is skilled enough to execute a half speed spike nonetheless. When hitting from a deeper attacking area with a slower ball velocity, it is almost certain that the ball will be directed to an area behind the attack line. Therefore, it is not necessary to defend the area ahead of the attack line in anticipation of the easier off-speed attack.

Once it is apparent to any one of the front row players that the opposition is unable to execute a spike attack, that player calls out "free" or "down" to signify either a free ball or a down ball situation. This call notifies the front row players that it is not necessary to block and that they are to move off the net to a position in the area of the attack line. Only the setter, whether a frontcourt or backcourt player, remains at the net. The remaining five players assume a formation that is very similar to the W serve reception formation. As illustrated in Figure 5.38, the free ball defense maintains

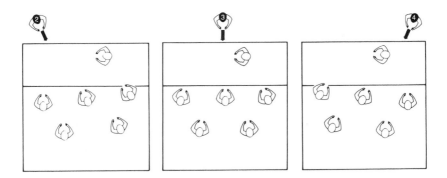

Figure 5.38 Although the basic formation remains the same, the focus of attention of the free ball defense changes according to which zone the attack comes from.

its basic W formation irrespective of which zone the attack comes from. Only the focus of attention of the free ball defense changes.

When facing opposition from any of the attacking zones, the free ball defense allows an efficient transition from defense to offense. Indeed, the free ball defense in many ways resembles the defense inherent in serve reception. Not only is the alignment of players very similar, but it is during these two phases of the game that many predetermined offensive plays (i.e., tandems, crosses, etc.) can be executed. The following section will illustrate in detail the movement and final positioning of players using a free ball defense in conjunction with specific defenses and offensive attacking systems.

6 Up Defense
Two-Hitter Attack With Set From #3

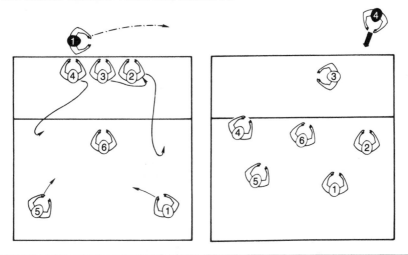

Figure 5.39 Direction of player movement in a free ball situation with player #3 responsible for setting the two-hitter attack.

All frontcourt players, with the exception of the designated setter (#3), fall off the net to the area of the attack line. The 6 up remains in position as the two remaining backcourt players (#1 and #5) move forward in anticipation of the free ball. The two backcourt players are responsible for defending the gaps between the three defenders on the attack line (Figure 5.39).

6 Up Defense
Two-Hitter Attack With Set From #2

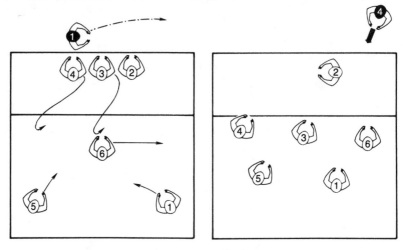

Figure 5.40   Direction of player movement in a free ball situation with player #2 responsible for setting the two-hitter attack.

In this situation player #2 remains at the net while the two remaining frontcourt players move back to the attack line. The 6 up moves laterally to the right to fill the gap created on the attack line when player #2 sets. The two backcourt players (#1 and #5) again move forward for the free ball and cover the gaps between the players on the attack line (Figure 5.40).

6 Up Defense
Three-Hitter Attack With Set From #6

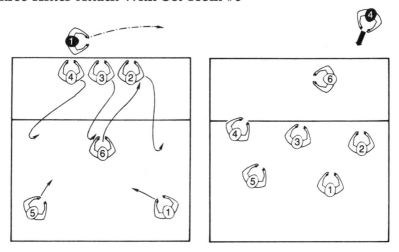

Figure 5.41 Direction of player movement in a free ball situation with player #6 responsible for penetrating and setting the three-hitter attack.

When preparing for a three-hitter attack off a free ball situation, all frontcourt players move off the net to the attack line. As the 6 up is the backcourt player closest to the net, he or she will be the designated setter. The setter moves up to zone #2 and assumes the responsibility of setting to the three available frontcourt hitters (#2, #3, and #4). The movements of players #1 and #5 are the same as in the two previous situations, with the same responsibilities (Figure 5.41).

6 Back Defense
Two-Hitter Attack With Set From #3

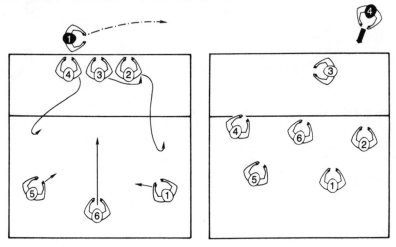

Figure 5.42 Direction of player movement in a free ball situation with player #3 responsible for setting the two-hitter attack.

All frontcourt players, with the exception of the designated setter (#3), fall off the net to the area of the attack line. The setter moves to zone #2 and the 6 back moves straight ahead to a position just behind the attack line in the center of the court. The two remaining backcourt players (#1 and #5) move forward in anticipation of the free ball. The two backcourt players are responsible for defending the gaps between the three defenders on the attack line (Figure 5.42).

6 Back Defense
Two-Hitter Attack With Set From #2

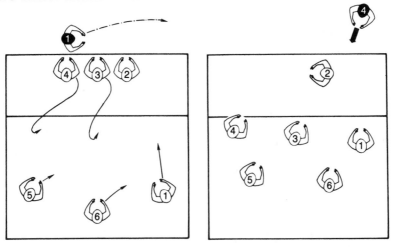

Figure 5.43 Direction of player movement in a free ball situation with player #2 responsible for setting the two-hitter attack.

In this situation the designated setter (#2) remains at the net in zone #2 while the two remaining frontcourt players (#3 and #4) move back to the attack line. Player #1 moves forward along the sideline to play the attack line area immediately behind the setter. The two remaining backcourt players (#5 and #6) move forward and to the right to fill in the midcourt gaps between the attack line players (Figure 5.43).

6 Back Defense
Three-Hitter Attack With Set From #1

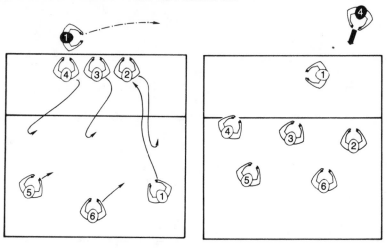

Figure 5.44 Direction of player movement in a free ball situation with player #1 responsible for penetrating and setting the three-hitter attack.

As with any three-hitter attack, the three frontcourt players are required to move off the net to an area on the attack line. In this situation player #1 is the backcourt player closest to the setting position. As a result player #1 will move forward between players #2 and #3 to the setting position in zone #2. In this case it is the setter's responsibility also to avoid interfering with the movement of players #2 and #3. The movement of players #5 and #6 is again forward and to the right to fill in the midcourt gaps (Figure 5.44).

Chapter 6

The Southpaw System

The purpose of this chapter is to expose the reader to a heretofore neglected system of volleyball team play. For any number of reasons, volleyball has progressed in many minor areas of strategy and tactics. It is hoped that the brief examples contained in this chapter will serve to initiate independent thinking on the part of the reader. In essence, with this groundwork of information it should be possible to develop a Southpaw System that will satisfy the unique needs of your team. However, use of the Southpaw System is not advocated for use by all coaches or teams. It must be weighed against the philosophy of the coach and the ability of the players. The purpose of this chapter is not to promote the Southpaw System as an ultimate system of volleyball team play but to expose the reader to an alternative system of play.

The system of play described in this chapter differs significantly from the conventional systems of play currently in use. Before discussing the technicalities of this unique system of play called the *Southpaw System*, it may be prudent to first define a conventional system.

The Conventional Systems

For the purpose of simple explanation, *conventional system* will refer to all those systems of play in which the setter's intended position is in the *right* third of the frontcourt. Figure 6.1 illustrates the intended positioning of frontcourt players within the bounds of a conventional system. The setter sets to the eligible hitters (outside hitter in zone #4 and middle hitter in zone #3) from the area of zone #2. Very nearly all systems of play in use at this time require the setter to set from this area.

The enormous popularity of this frontcourt configuration may be the result of several factors. Perhaps it is due to the fact that the majority of players are right-handed, in which case the conventional systems allow for the preferable outside attack. Maybe it is due to the fact that, traditionally, the set has always been executed from either the middle or the right third of the frontcourt. Perhaps it has been used simply because everybody else uses it. In the final analysis, this in fact may prove to be the preeminent reason for employing the use of conventional right side set systems of play. As a generalization, coaches tend to coach as they themselves have been coached or as they have been taught to coach, the result of this being that impetus for change is often long in coming.

Figure 6.1 The intended positioning of frontcourt players when using a conventional system. Note the setter positioned in zone #2 in the right third of the frontcourt.

Regardless of the popularity and currently widespread use of these conventional systems of play, there are situations in which they simply are not adequate. Therefore an alternative must be sought. The Southpaw System was born out of necessity rather than out of a desire for unwarranted change; this system has been designed to satisfy the specific needs of teams for which a conventional system of play is either not adequate or not desired.

The Southpaw System

Very simply, the Southpaw System is a system of play in which the setter's intended position is in the *left* rather than the right third of the frontcourt (Figure 6.2). The system has been so named to correspond with the fact that, when in use, the offense is directed from the left side of the frontcourt. In fact, the positioning of the frontcourt players is a mirror image of the usual positions of a conventional system. In the Southpaw System, the setter sets from zone #4 to either the middle hitter in zone #3 or the outside hitter in zone #2. Not only is the alignment of players unique but so too are the intended objectives of the system.

Figure 6.2 Intended positioning of frontcourt players when using the Southpaw System. Note the setter positioned in the left third of the frontcourt (zone #4).

Why Use It?

This system can and perhaps should be used for either of two very distinct reasons, one being primarily defensive and the other basically offensive in nature. Therefore, we have two distinct considerations that must be confronted prior to the implementation of this system.

Defensive Consideration

This consideration is relative to the defensive blocking ability of the frontcourt setter. In a conventional defensive alignment, the frontcourt setter is positioned in zone #2 (Figure 6.1). In this position, the setter is required to block against the opposition's outside power hitter. If the frontcourt setter were physically unable to provide a defensive block against the opposition's outside hitter (due to a lack of height or jumping ability), the opposing team would accrue a marked advantage. The unfortunate result of this would be the opposition's ability to score easy kills over the short and ineffective block of the frontcourt setter.

A viable solution to this dilemma is to employ the use of the Southpaw System. The frontcourt setter then would be positioned in zone #4, where the frequency of opposition attack is significantly decreased, and the frontcourt hitter would be positioned in zone #2 opposite the opposition's outside hitter. Ultimately, the use of this system may do little to increase offensive power, but it will dramatically increase your team's potential to defend against the outside attack of the opposition.

Offensive Consideration

This consideration deals specifically with teams having a large number of left-handed hitters. Although typically difficult to defend, left-handed hitters are offensively disadvantaged in having to play within the conventional systems of play. In these systems, a left-handed hitter must contact the set ball as it passes across his or her body. This offside attack is generally not as effective as the onside attack, in which the set ball approaches from the same side as the hitter's striking arm. Therefore, to enable the preferred onside attack by left-handed hitters, a distinctly different yet viable system of play must be employed.

The Southpaw System greatly improves the offensive capabilities of the left-handed hitters by positioning the setter in an area to the left of the two primary hitters (middle hitter and outside hitter). In this alignment, the middle and outside hitters receive the preferred onside sets. An additional offensive advantage is accrued through the many different and unique angles of attack available to the left-handed hitters within this system of play.

Advantages and Disadvantages

As with any system of play, the Southpaw System has advantages and disadvantages. It is this balance of advantages and disadvantages that must be carefully studied and assessed. Only if the advantages to your team outweigh the disadvantages should this system of play be implemented.

Advantages

- The success of the opposition's outside attack (from the opposition's zone #4) is significantly reduced as a result of the larger and more effective block formed by the middle and outside hitters.
- Left-handed hitters benefit greatly from this system in that they receive the preferred onside pass from the setter.
- Offensively, all hitters will have different angles of attack that the opposition will be forced to defend against. In many instances, the opposition will not be adequately prepared to defend against these uncommon angles of attack, thereby advantaging your offensive hitters.
- Right-handed setters are in a position to easily execute a quick hit on a second pass. Positioned in zone #4, the frontcourt setter can easily turn toward the net, as the second pass approaches his or her position, and contact the ball powerfully with his or her right (hitting) hand, for a quick hit.
- The ability of your team to switch back and forth between conventional systems (right side set) and the Southpaw System (left side set) effectively doubles the offensive options available to your team. This also doubles the number of possible attacks the opposition must be prepared to defend.
- With the ability to switch between conventional systems and the Southpaw System also comes the ability to manipulate the

opposition. The opposition must be prepared to defend against your team's ability to switch between systems and therefore they will be reacting to your direction. Consequently, your team will be in the driver's seat, directing the flow and tempo of the game.

- The element of surprise is clearly at your disposal.

Disadvantages

- Generally, your frontcourt outside hitter (zone #2) also faces a larger block formed by the opposition's middle and outside hitters.
- Right-handed hitters are required to hit from the less effective offside position.
- Defensively, most middle and outside attacks are received crosscourt (i.e., directed diagonally into the area of zone #5), forcing the backcourt defender in that area to receive and execute a pass at a refractory angle to the setter in zone #4 (refer to Chapter 4, Figure 4.6). As described in Chapter 4, this pass is somewhat more difficult to execute than a return pass in the same diagonal direction to zone #2.
- This system requires a great deal of mental preparation and concentration on the part of the players.

The Southpaw System in Play

For the purpose of simplicity, the remainder of this chapter will focus on the use of the 6 up defense and the 4-2 offense within the confines of the Southpaw System. It must be understood, however, that any combination of defensive and offensive systems may be accommodated within the Southpaw System. This can easily be accomplished by relating the principles of the Southpaw System to the information contained in the preceding chapters. Were the Southpaw System to be extensively explained, it could well be the subject of yet another book.

Offensive Serve/Defense

It is during the offensive serve that the positions of the Southpaw System are most easily assumed. During the seconds while the served ball travels to the opposite court and the opposition prepares its attack, the players may easily move to their intended positions. Figure 6.3 illustrates the three rotations that will repetitively occur when using a 6 up defense in conjunction with a 4-2 offense. Each of the three rotations is diagramed showing the initial positioning of players [Figure 6.3 (i), (iv), and (vii)], direction of player movement [Figure 6.3 (ii), (v), and (viii)], and the final positioning of players [Figure 6.3 (iii), (vi), and (ix)].

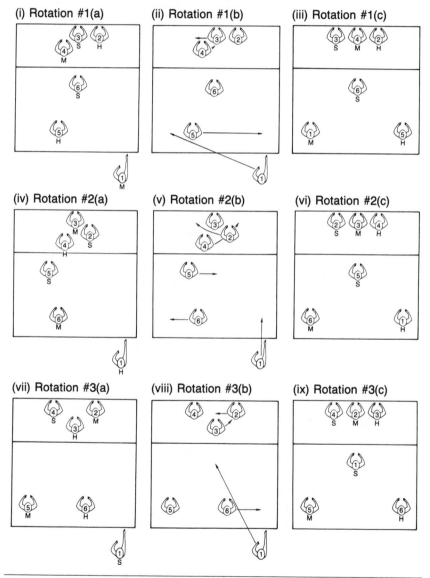

Figure 6.3 (i)-(ix) Initial positioning (i), (iv), and (vii), direction of movement (ii), (v), and (viii), and final positioning (iii), (vi), and (ix) of players through each of the first three offensive serve rotations.

It is also apparent in Figure 6.3 that the guidelines pertaining to the 6 up defensive system are adhered to. In each instance, the back-court setter moves to a final position in the 6 up defense closest to the frontcourt setter's position. From this position, he or she may penetrate to the frontcourt setter's position in zone #4 to set to a three-hitter attack. In all respects, the 6 up defense is executed in the same manner within the Southpaw System as it would be in any conventional system. The responsibilities of each position within the 6 up defense remain the same regardless of the desig-nation of the players occupying the positions.

Serve Reception

It is during the serve reception phase of play that the Southpaw System may be most effective. Prior to the serve, the penetrating setter decides whether to use a conventional system of play or the Southpaw System. If choosing the former, he or she penetrates to the *right* frontcourt setter's position. If choosing the latter, he or she penetrates to the *left* frontcourt setter's position. The pos-sibility of choosing between either of the two systems illustrates the numerous options available to a team that has mastered the Southpaw System.

In serve reception also, there are three distinct and repetitive ro-tations, the first of which is diagramed in Figure 6.4. In this W serve reception formation, the backcourt setter (player #6) begins in an initial position slightly behind and to the right of the frontcourt setter (player #3). From this initial position, the backcourt setter appears to be preparing to penetrate to the conventional right side setter's position (zone #2). However, the setter instead steps across behind player #3 and then moves forward to a position in the left frontcourt (zone #4). In this first rotation, either the right or left side setter's position is accessible to the penetrating setter. The op-position is clearly disadvantaged in that it is unaware of the set-ter's intention until the served ball has been contacted. This creates a situation in which you have manipulated your opponent by ef-fectively disguising your intensions, thus minimizing any antici-pation on the part of the opposing team.

The second rotation provides the easiest and most direct route for the backcourt setter (player #5) to penetrate to the left front-court setter's position (Figure 6.5). Positioning behind and to the

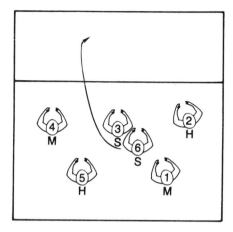

Figure 6.4 Backcourt setter (#6) penetrating to zone #4 to set the offense in the Southpaw System.

right of player #4, the penetrating setter again appears to be preparing to move to the conventional right side setter's position. In a conventional system, however, the setter is required to cross the entire width of the frontcourt, a time consuming path. Instead, the backcourt setter simply moves forward to zone #4, consistent with the concepts of the Southpaw System.

The third rotation offers the possibility of several unique serve reception formations. One possibility may be to have the backcourt

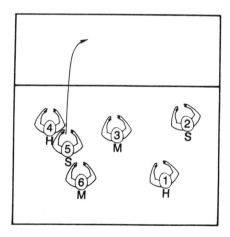

Figure 6.5 Backcourt setter (#5) penetrating to the left frontcourt setter's position.

setter (player #1) penetrate directly to the conventional right side setter's position (Figure 6.6). This would certainly be the easiest and least confusing of the options. Conversely, the backcourt setter may choose instead to penetrate to the left side setter's position (Figure 6.7). This, however, would be very time consuming because the setter must again cross the entire width of the frontcourt.

One option may be to have the frontcourt setter move forward to set (Figure 6.8). In this instance, players #4, #5, #6, and #1 would each move clockwise one position. This movement would be executed quickly and immediately prior to the opposition's serve. In order for this play to be effective, it is imperative that the players move in unison, on the setter's signal, to their designated positions. Although this would appear to be a slow and difficult formation for serve reception, it is in fact relatively easy to execute. This particular option, however, may not prove beneficial when weighing its advantages against the disadvantages. If this is the case, there are still other alternatives for serve reception in this rotation.

Figure 6.9 illustrates what would be the end product of the aforementioned serve reception formation. If the previous formation is deemed too risky, it is possible to begin with players initially positioned in this formation. This formation is extremely safe, as no extraneous player movement is required. However, there is a trade-

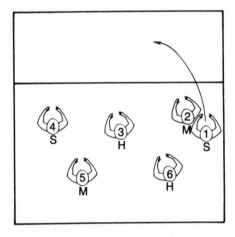

Figure 6.6 Backcourt setter (#1) penetrating to the conventional right side set position.

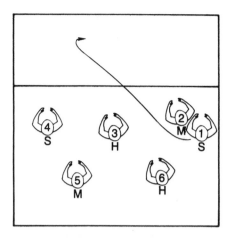

Figure 6.7 Backcourt setter (#1) penetrating to the left frontcourt setter's position in accordance with the Southpaw System.

off in that the opposition will be very aware that your team is setting from the left side setter's position to a two-hitter offensive attack. This too can be hidden by using yet another serve reception formation in this particular rotation.

Figure 6.10 illustrates a formation in which it appears that player #5 will be penetrating to set to a three-hitter attack. Instead, however, the frontcourt setter (player #4) moves forward to the left side

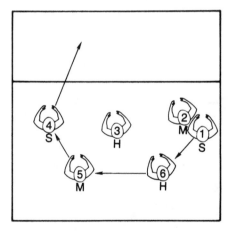

Figure 6.8 The direction of movement as four of the receiving players switch positions so that player #4 may move ahead to the left frontcourt setter's position.

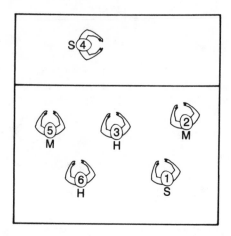

Figure 6.9 Alignment of players when player #4 is initially positioned in the left frontcourt setter's position.

setter's position to set to a two-hitter attack. The opposition anticipates the possibility of having to defend three eligible hitters and spreads out the defense.

It should be very apparent that there are numerous formation possibilities for serve reception at this point in the rotation. In fact, all of the formations that have been described in this chapter comprise less than half of the possible serve reception formations available when using the Southpaw System. This should serve as an

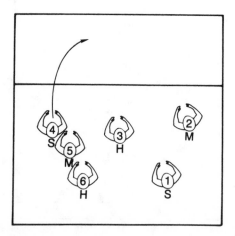

Figure 6.10 Backcourt player #5 faking penetration as frontcourt player #4 moves forward to the left side setter's position.

example of just how complex the Southpaw System can become when fully explored.

Offense

The offense of the Southpaw System is executed in basically the same manner as when using a conventional system. The one major difference is that the intended positioning of frontcourt players is reversed so that the setter is in zone #4 while the outside hitter and middle hitter are in zones #2 and #3 respectively (Figure 6.11). The intended positioning of backcourt players corresponds to the guidelines of the 6 up defense (Figure 6.11). From these basic offensive positions within the Southpaw System, all combinations of offensive attacks are possible. This includes all offensive systems (i.e., 5-1, 3-3, etc.), all multiple offenses (i.e., tandem, cross, etc.), all quick attacks (i.e., A quick, shoot, etc.), and any combinations of these. All of the information contained in Chapter 5 can easily be applied to the Southpaw System, if the reader has an appreciation of the concepts inherent in that system.

It is hoped that the brief examples contained in this chapter will serve to initiate independent thinking on the part of the reader. In essence, with this groundwork of information it should be possible to develop a Southpaw System that will satisfy the unique needs of your team. However, use of the Southpaw System is not

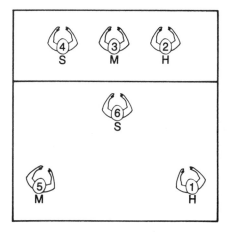

Figure 6.11 Basic offensive alignment of players when using the Southpaw System.

advocated for use by all coaches or teams. It must be weighed against the philosophy of the coach and the ability of the players. The purpose of this chapter is not to promote the Southpaw System as an ultimate system of volleyball team play but to expose the reader to an alternative system of play.

Epilogue

Through this book I have endeavored to present the basic strategies and systems of play involved in the game of volleyball. It should be clearly understood that the systems of play described here merely scratch the surface of possibilities available. From this introduction, however, it will be possible for you to apply some of these principles to more complex strategies and systems of play.

Ultimately, at the elite levels of play, there are systems of play that are so advanced and so complex that literally years of practice are required to perfect them. The most elite level of volleyball has grown so much, that more diverse and unique systems of play must be developed in order to accommodate the increasingly skilled athletes who now participate. Between this level and that of basic strategy lie a myriad of intermediate-level systems of play.

This book, then, should not be perceived as the definitive word on volleyball strategy, but rather it should serve as the basis from which you further develop the strategy of the game. To limit your knowledge and application of volleyball systems and strategy to what is contained in this book would defeat the book's intended purpose. It is my hope that you use this material as a starting point from which you may develop more advanced and more complex systems of team play. The possibilities are limited only by your creativity and imagination.

Inasmuch as you are the future of volleyball, it follows that you owe a responsibility to the growth of volleyball. This responsibility should not be accepted grudgingly; rather, it should be welcomed as an opportunity to make an indelible and yet very personal contribution to the development of the game.

Glossary

Area Block. A blocking system in which a player or players set up a block to disallow the opposition's hitter from hitting to a specific area of the defensive court.

Attack. Refers to the offensive play(s) of a team.

Attack Coverage. That phase of play in which the players of the offensive or attacking team position themselves in a defensive alignment behind the hitter while the attack is in process.

Attack Line. That court marking which runs across the full width of the court, parallel to, and three meters behind, the net.

Backcourt. That area of the court bounded by the attack line, the baseline, and each of the sidelines.

Baseline. (Also Endline) The court boundary that joins each of the sidelines at either end of the court area.

Block. The individual play in which the frontcourt player(s) of the defensive team jump and, with arms extended upwards, stop the hit ball of the opposition's attacker.

Center Line. The court marking that runs below and parallel to the net from sideline to sideline.

Crosscourt Attack. An attack in which the ball is hit diagonally crosscourt (e.g., from offensive zone #4 to defensive zone #5).

Crosscourt Block. An area block in which the blocker(s) deny the attacker a crosscourt hit.

Cup Serve Reception. A serve reception formation in which there are four receivers positioned in a cup formation. This is an offense oriented system of serve reception.

Cut Back Attack. An attack in which the offensive middle hitter spikes the ball back against his or her direction of attack from offensive zone #3 to defensive zones #1 or #2.

Cut Back Block. An area block in which the defensive blocker(s) deny the opposition's middle hitter a cut back attack hit.

Defense. That phase of play in which a team does not have possession of the ball.

Dig. The action of a defensive player in which a spike is received with an underhand pass, prior to the ball's contact with the floor.

Down Ball. A play in which the opposition's third contact of the ball is such that a spike can be executed only from an area deep in the court and well away from the net.

Eligible Hitter. Any player whose initial position in any given rotation is in the frontcourt (i.e., positions #4, #3, and #2).

Fake Penetration. An instance in which a backcourt player, usually a setter, fakes or feigns an attempt to move forward to the frontcourt.

Free Ball. A play in which the opposition's third contact of the ball is such that it will be unable to spike the ball but must instead pass the ball easily over the net.

Frontcourt. That area of the court bounded by the attack line, the center line, and each of the sidelines.

Kill. A spike that cannot be played by the opposition, resulting in a point or side out.

Line Block. An area block in which the blocker(s) deny the attacker a hit straight down the sideline.

Multiple Offense. An offensive attack that involves three eligible front row hitters in a combination of attacks and fake attacks.

Offense. That phase of play in which a team has possession of the ball.

Offensive Systems. Systems of offense that include various combinations of hitters and setters. These offensive systems are referred to numerically according to the combination of hitters and setters. For example, in a 4-2 offensive system there are four hitters and two setters, in a 5-1 system there are five hitters and only one setter.

Offside Attack. An attack that is directed from zone #2 behind the setter who is also in zone #2. This is referred to as an offside or weakside attack due to the fact that the majority of offensive attacks are directed from zones #4 and #3 in front of the setter rather than from zone #2 behind the setter.

Onside Attack. An attack that is directed from positions #4 or #3 when the setter is setting from position #2. The onside or strong side is the side in which the two primary hitters, #4 and #3, are in front of the setter, who is facing them in zone #2.

Penetration. The movement of a backcourt player, usually a setter, who is moving forward to a position in the frontcourt.

Player to Player Block. A blocking system in which each defensive blocking player is assigned to block against one particular opponent, usually the opponent who is lined up opposite him or her.

Quick Sets. Those sets made by the setter to a hitter who is already in motion to the net. The purpose of a quick set is to catch the opposition off guard with its low arc and decreased distance from setter to hitter.

Rotational Order. The numerical description of player positioning. For example, the server is referred to as player #1 or playing in position #1 (also zone #1). The player positioned at the net in front of player #1 is player #2 or is in position #2 (also zone #2). This numbering system continues in a counterclockwise fashion for positions (zones) #1 through #6.

Serve. That phase of play in which action is initiated with a single contact of the ball by the server (player #1), directly over the net to the opposition.

Serve Reception. That phase of play in which a team receives the serve of the opposition.

Service Area. The area behind and parallel to the baseline that extends from the right sideline 3 meters along the baseline. It is from within this area that the serve is initiated.

Setter. The player or players whose designated responsibility is to pass the ball to the hitter(s) so that a spike may be executed.

Sideline. The court marking that encloses each of the two sides of the court by joining the baselines.

Side Out. The winning of a rally by the team who received the serve. As a score can be made only when serving, the receiving team in essence scores a side out.

Southpaw System. A complete system of play in which the positioning of the setter is in the left side of the frontcourt rather than the more common right side of the frontcourt.

Spike. The action of hitting the ball with an overhand motion on a downward trajectory over the net at the opposition.

Switching. The movement of players who are exchanging or changing positions within the original rotational order.

Three-Hitter Attack. An attack in which there are three eligible frontcourt hitters.

Two-Hitter Attack. An attack in which there are two eligible frontcourt hitters.

W Serve Reception. A serve reception formation in which there are five receivers positioned in a W formation. Each of the five players represents one of the five points that make up the letter W. This is a defense oriented system of serve reception.

Wipe-Off. An offensive attack in which the ball is hit such that it will be redirected off the hands of the defensive blocker and fall to an area outside of the playing court or to an area where it cannot be played by the defense.

6 Back Defense. A defensive system based on the alignment of player #6 who is positioned close to the baseline behind and between players #5 and #1.

6 Up Defense. A defensive system based on the alignment of player #6 who is positioned close to the attack line between and in front of players #5 and #1.

Further Reading

Fraser, S. (1985). The southpaw system, *Athletic Journal*, **65**(7), 22-25.

Fraser, S. (1983). What's left of the right set?, *Coaching Review*, **6**, 53-54.

Mosher, M. (1979). Training of a quick attack hitter, *C.V.A. Conductors Manual—Level 3*, pp. 2.46-2.48.

Prsala, J., & Hoyle, J. (1982). *Volleyball for everybody*. Halifax: Ford.

Sawula, L. (1979, December). Variations of 6-up and 6-back defensive systems, *C.V.A. Conductors Manual*, pp. 3.16-3.23.

Scates, A. (1979). *Winning volleyball*. Boston: Allyn and Bacon.

Tennant, M. (1977). *Volleyball team play*. Ottawa: Canadian Volleyball Association.

About the Author

STEPHEN D. FRASER

Steve Fraser holds a degree in physical education from Dalhousie University in Halifax, Nova Scotia, and is a certified coach of volleyball, basketball, hockey, and soccer. He has coached junior high, high school, and college volleyball and has been a developmental coordinator with Sport Nova Scotia. In addition to *Strategies for Competitive Volleyball*, Steve has authored several articles for volleyball publications. He is a member of the Royal Canadian Air Force and lives with his wife, Lisa, in Halifax.